Words of Wisdom for Teens

THE COMPLETE COLLECTION

Books 1 to 3

Jacqui Letran

DUNEDIN, FLORIDA

Publisher's Cataloging-In-Publication Data

Names: Letran, Jacqui.
Title: Words of Wisdom for Teens: The Complete Collection / Jacqui Letran.
Description: 1st edition. | Dunedin, Florida: A Healed Mind, [2021] | Series: Words of wisdom for teens series; complete series| Interest age level: 12 and up.
Identifiers: ISBN 978-1-952719-12-7 (hardcover) ISBN 978-1-952719-10-3 (paperback)

Subjects: LCSH: Adolescent psychology. | Teenagers--Attitudes. | Happiness in adolescence. | Emotions in adolescence. | Self-help techniques for teenagers.
Classification: LCC BF724.L48 2016 (print) | LCC BF724 (e-book) | DDC 155.5--dc23

Table of Contents

Book Three: Jump-Start Your Confidence

5 Simple Steps to Manage Your Mood

A Guide for Teen Girls: How to Let Go of
Negative Feelings and Create a Happy
Relationship with Yourself and Others

Book 1 of 3 from the

Words of Wisdom for Teens Series

Jacqui Letran

DUNEDIN, FLORIDA

Table of Contents

CHAPTER ONE

5 Simple Questions to Reclaim Your Happiness!

A re you frustrated because one bad event can ruin your entire day or maybe even your entire week? Does it seem like no matter what you try to do, you just can't seem to shake those negative thoughts and feelings? Instead of being able to let go of things easily, do you often hang on to things long after everyone else seems to have forgotten about them?

If you answered "yes" to these questions, you are not alone. Many people have a hard time letting things go. Instead, when something goes wrong, they replay that scenario over and over in their head, causing them to feel worse about themselves or worse about the other person, or people involved.

Think about the last argument you had with someone that really bothered you. What was that like? Did you replay the argument over and over and beating yourself up for all the things you wished you had done or said differently? Did you make up conversations that didn't even take place and feeling even more upset? Did you think about other similar situations and spiraling downward into sadness, anger, or pain?

Let's say that after the argument had taken place, you wanted to patch things up. Were you able to shake those negativities so you could do what you wanted to do, or were you weighed down and held back by your emotions? Did you feel in control of your emotions or did you feel as if your emotions were controlling you?

For many people, shaking those negative feelings is difficult even when they want to let things go. This is because they don't understand just how much power and control, they do have over their emotions. Maybe this is where you are right now.

Understanding your feelings and knowing what to do with them may seem like a difficult task right now. However, with the right tools, this task can become manageable and even easy. When you use the 5 simple questions to guide you, you can understand and release your unwanted feelings easily so you can focus on rebuilding or strengthening your relationships and reclaiming your happiness.

You can use these same 5 simple questions to help you regain your happiness whether your disagreement is with a parent, a friend, or even with yourself.

To illustrate how you can use these 5 simple questions, let's look at a scenario that happened between my sixteen-year-old client, Amie, and her mother, Beth.

Beth is at home anxiously waiting for her daughter, Amie, to return. It is 10 p.m., which is thirty minutes past Amie's curfew. Amie is late yet again. Beth continues to watch the clock. Minutes feel like hours. Beth becomes angrier. Beth can't understand why Amie continues to violate her curfew and disrespect her rules.

The fights between Beth and Amie have been escalating these past few months. After their last major argument, Beth grounded Amie for two weeks because Amie returned home three hours late. Amie did her best not to talk to Beth for the entire two weeks. When forced to interact, Amie limited her answers to one or two words. The anger, frustration, and resentment between Beth and Amie continued to grow.

In yet another fight, the following week, Amie screamed at Beth, accusing her of being unreasonable, unfair, and too strict with the curfew. Between sobs, Amie pleaded with Beth to see that she was grown up. Amie asked for some understanding, trust, and respect for her ability to make good decisions for herself.

Like many previous fights, this one ended up with Amie angrily stomping off to her room and slamming her door while Beth stood there feeling frustrated and helpless.

Since the last fight, Beth has been trying to be more lenient when Amie breaks curfew. Instead of yelling at Amie and grounding her, Beth does her best to calmly remind Amie of her curfew. Although Beth felt angry and disrespected inside, outwardly she stays in control and tells Amie, "I am not happy when you come home late. It would be nice if you came home at 10 p.m. I could trust and respect your decisions more that way." Noticing her anger rising, Beth leaves the house and goes for a walk to calm herself down. This happened at least four times in the previous two weeks.

Beth thinks she is handling herself well, but the anger and resentment haven't gone away, in fact, it's been steadily rising. Today, she can no longer contain herself. As the *minutes continue to pass, her anger builds. Beth recalls all the times that Amie has violated her trust or in any way acted entitled or ungrateful. Beth becomes livid.*

The moment Amie walks in the house, Beth rages at Amie, telling her how she is sick and tired of being disrespected. She adds, "I raised a much better daughter than you. I don't know what I did to deserve this. You are selfish, untrustworthy, and all you do is cause me pain."

Amie stands speechless and confused about what is happening. It's only 10:40 p.m., twenty minutes earlier than previous times when she came home at 11 p.m. to a calm and reasonable mother.

As you can imagine, neither mother nor daughter is happy with the exchange. Both feel angry and disappointed.

Throughout this book, we will examine how Beth and Amie used the 5 simple questions to reclaim happiness after their fight.

REMEMBER: *While helpful, these 5 questions are not meant to replace professional help. If your situation is difficult to handle, or you don't know how to proceed, please talk to your parents or a trusted adult and ask for help.*

CHAPTER TWO

Question 1:
What Am I Feeling?

Identifying your emotions is an important first step to reclaiming your happiness. By identifying your emotion, you can evaluate it and decide what to do with it. Too often, we over-generalize our emotional state as "bad" or "mad." In reality, feeling "bad" has many meanings. When you say, "I feel bad," you could mean "I feel sad," or "I feel lonely," or maybe, "I feel anxious," or even "I feel guilty." Similarly, "I am mad," could mean, "I am disappointed," or "I am irritated," or maybe "I am annoyed," or even "I am furious."

When you use a general word to express your emotions repeatedly, that term (and emotion) becomes stronger and feels heavier and heavier. This makes it more difficult to change your emotional state or let go of your unwanted feelings. When you identify the specific emotion, it becomes smaller, lighter, and much easier to let go.

Here's an example to help you understand this idea clearly. Imagine a moving day—the day you pack your household in preparation to move. Imagine putting everything from your bedroom (your bed, a dresser, a closet full of clothes, etc.)

into one gigantic box and label it "bedroom." Would you be able to move the box easily? Would it be easy or difficult to find individual items within this box quickly? When you need to retrieve an item and look inside that box, does it look easy—or is it overwhelming or daunting?

Instead of one gigantic box, what if you separated your belongings into many little boxes and labeled them correctly? Imagine having 20-30 clearly labelled boxes: winter clothes, shoes, books, games, and so on. If you need to move one of those boxes, would you be able to move it easily? What if you need to find a pair of shoes? Wouldn't it be easy to grab the box labeled "shoes" and open it?

The same is true with your emotions. When you pack your emotions under one big label, they remain cluttered, heavy, and unmanageable. Instead, take a second to identify your emotions and decide what you want to do with them.

It's easy for Beth and Amie to blame the other person to feel justified in their anger. However, when they looked inward, they discovered a range of emotions and options for handling them.

Beth reported feeling angry, disrespected, disappointed, resentful, violated, frustrated, unloved, misunderstood, taken advantage of, and unappreciated.

Amie reported feeling confused, angry, annoyed, disappointed, sad, afraid, helpless, unloved, accused, misunderstood, and frustrated.

Beth discovered her strongest emotions were feeling disrespected and taken advantage of, while Amie felt confused and frustrated.

REMEMBER: *When you identify your specific emotion, it becomes smaller, lighter, and much easier to let go.*

Did you know that there are over several hundred words in the English dictionary to describe emotions? Yet, most people use only eight to ten words to describe how they feel. The words I most often hear in my practice when I ask a client to describe how they feel about their problems are: bad, sad, angry, hurt, disappointed, anxious, and scared.

When you use one word to express an emotion repeatedly, that emotion feels big and difficult to change. To help you let go of a negative emotion easier, get specific with your words and challenge yourself to use a different label each time. Get creative, have fun, and get ready to be amazed to discover just how much control you do have over your emotions.

On the next few pages are a list of common emotions. This is not a complete list of all emotions, just a select few to get you to think about different ways to express yourself. On the list, I left out many words that might make you feel worse because they imply judgment or suggest that something is wrong with you. The idea is to keep your emotion as light as you can while expressing your feelings. This will help your mind release it faster.

Accused	Afraid	Aggravated
Aggressive	Agitated	Alienated
Alone	Ambivalent	Annoyed
Antsy	Anxious	Apprehensive
Attacked	Awkward	Baffled
Beat	Bitter	Blamed
Bleak	Blocked	Bored
Bothered	Bruised	Bummed
Burdened	Burned	Cheated
Combative	Concerned	Conflicted
Confused	Crabby	Cranky
Criticized	Cross	Crummy
Crushed	Deceived	Defeated
Defenseless	Deflated	Deprived
Despair	Detached	Disappointed
Disconnected	Discouraged	Disgruntled
Disillusioned	Dismay	Disorganized
Displeased	Disrespected	Dissatisfied
Distress	Disturbed	Doubtful
Down	Drained	Dread
Edgy	Embarrassed	Empty
Enraged	Excluded	Exhausted
Fear or fearful	Fidgety	Flustered
Forced	Fragile	Framed
Frantic	Frightened	Frustrated
Furious	Gloomy	Grouchy
Grumpy	Guarded	Guilty
Gullible	Heated	Heavy
Helpless	Hesitant	Hindered
Horrible	Horrified	Hostile

Humbled	Hurt	Icky
Ignored	Impatient	Inconvenienced
Indecisive	Indifference	Ineffective
Inhibited	Insecure	Insulted
Invalidated	Irked	Irrational
Irritated	Isolated	Jaded
Jealous	Judged	Jumpy
Lazy	Leery	Limited
Lonely	Loopy	Lost
Low	Mad	Manipulated
Meek	Miserable	Misled
Mistaken	Misunderstood	Moody
Neglected	Nervous	Numb
Offended	Overwhelmed	Perplexed
Pissed	Pooped	Pressured
Provoked	Puzzled	Rattled
Regretful	Resentful	Responsible
Restless	Ridiculed	Ridiculous
Robbed	Ruffled	Scared
Self-Conscious	Sensitive	Sheepish
Shocked	Shook up	Sick
Skeptical	Sorrow	Sorry
Spiteful	Startled	Strained
Stressed	Stuck	Stumped
Suppressed	Suspicious	Tense
Terrified	Threatened	Thrown
Trapped	Uncertain	Undermined
Unhappy	Unhinged	Unsure
Uptight	Vulnerable	Weigh down
Wired	Withdrawn	Worn

Let's have some fun with slang words from
urbandictionary.com

Bent	Blown	Butt-hurt
Cheesed-off	Cut	Driddy
Durpy	Furt	Limp
Peeved	Petro	Poxy
Salty	Shut-down	Skerred
Stumb	Wacked	Wrecked

It's your turn to come up with other words you can use to describe your negative emotions. Think of words you use and words you have heard other people use and make your own list. You can even make up words if you like. I have a client, Helen, who used to say, "I'm so stupid," whenever she made a mistake, and that statement made her feel terrible about herself. After going through this exercise, Helen decided to make up her own words and now says, "Abba tea toe tea" and laughs it off whenever she makes a mistake. Those words she made up make no sense and are so funny, she and others can't help but shake it off and move on. In fact, a few of her friends are now using the same words to keep things light so they, too, can move on.

CHAPTER THREE

Question 2:
Why Do I Feel This Way?

Answering this question will give you insight into your emotions and insight into yourself. As with the first question, this question allows you to sort your emotions and helps you to release the emotion that's holding you back so you can focus on reclaiming your happiness.

How many times have you said, "I don't know why I feel [insert your emotion here]? I just do." Or maybe you've said, "I am really anxious right now, but I don't know why."

When you say, "I don't know why," in response to someone's question about your feelings, it may be an automatic answer because you don't want to talk about it. Or, perhaps, you really don't understand your feelings because you haven't stopped to examine them.

When you respond in this manner, you are basically claiming, "I am powerless. My feelings are beyond my understanding and control." By not understanding why you feel the way you do, you become a victim of your feelings. You also place yourself in a situation of being powerless to change it.

You might wonder, "But I really don't know why I feel the way I do. Does that mean I am powerless?" Not at all. If you stop and look inward, you will find the reason for why you feel the way you do.

In life, there are only three causes for upset feelings, and they are very simple:

1. Unmet expectations
2. Thwarted intentions: something that stops or keeps you from what you've intended to do or have happened
3. A miscommunication or misunderstanding that leads to #1 or #2 above

Understanding the causes of your upset feelings will help you break free from your burden.

The next time you are having a relationship challenge, take a deep breath in and ask yourself:

1. What were my expectations in this situation and were they met?
2. Were my expectations realistic for this situation? Remember, just because you want things a certain way, doesn't mean it's realistic.
3. What were my intentions and did something happen that prevented me from completing my intentions?
4. Did I communicate my expectations or intentions to others clearly?
5. Did I understand the expectations or intentions of the other person(s)?

When you answer these questions honestly, you will find the reason for your upset feeling. Once you identify your emotion and the reason behind it, you reclaim your power to do something about it. From a place of understanding and strength, you can decide on a course of action that is best suited to create the results you want.

Beth feels entitled to her sense of being disrespected and taken advantage of. After all, Amie knew her curfew time but continued to disrespect it. Beth has tried to avoid a fight by speaking calmly to Amie, but rather than appreciating this, Amie took advantage of her kindness and continued to show a lack of care.

When Beth stops to reflect on the reasons for her upset feeling, she discovers:

1. *She expected Amie to follow the previously stated curfew time, and her expectation was not met.*

2. *She felt her expectation was realistic for this situation.*

3. *Her intention was to avoid a fight. Amie's continued disrespect made it hard for her to continue to be kind and understanding.*

4. *She realized she did not communicate her expectations clearly. She realized when she said, "I am not happy when you come home late. It would be nice if you came home at 10 p.m. I could trust and respect your decisions more that way," without enforcing previous consequences, she opened up the situation for interpretation and confusion.*

5. *She was not aware of Amie's expectations or intentions.*

Amie feels confused and frustrated about what happened. She doesn't understand why her mom is enraged and accuses her of being selfish, untrustworthy, and causing her pain when she made a conscious decision to make her mom proud tonight. Amie thought they came to a new understanding about her curfew after the last fight when she begged her mom for some leeway. Since her mom started acting "cool" when Amie came home at 11 p.m., Amie assumed that was the new curfew time. Tonight, she decided to surprise her mom by coming home early.

When Amie examines her feelings, she discovered:

1. *She expected her mom to be happy that she came home twenty minutes earlier than she had been lately.*

2. *She came home a little earlier than 11 p.m. to show her mom she could be responsible for her decisions. She was proud of herself for making this decision and was expecting her mom to show appreciation and encouragement.*

3. *She did not communicate her intentions or expectations. She never confirmed the new curfew time. She was just happy that they were not fighting anymore and that her mother was beginning to see her as capable of making smart decisions for herself.*

Amie realizes that she did not fully understand her mom's expectations. Even though her mom had said, "It would be nice if you came home by 10 p.m.," Amie decided that was only a guideline since there were no consequences like before.

REMEMBER: *There are only three causes for upset feelings: unmet expectations, thwarted intentions, and miscommunication.*

Once you identify your emotion and the reason behind it, you reclaim your power to change. From a place of strength, you can decide on a course of action that is best suited to create your desired results.

CHAPTER FOUR

Question 3:
Is This Emotion Useful for Any Reason?

So many emotions have no purpose other than to burden you and keep you stuck in a cycle of misery or pain. Other emotions have awesome purposes and can lead you down the path to your greatest and happiest self.

Have you ever known someone who is highly sensitive and cries easily when they are upset? What about someone who gets angry at the slightest thing? How about a person who is so anxious that it's difficult for them to do things that are simple for most people? Maybe you know someone like that, or maybe that someone is you, and you don't know what to do. Perhaps you've been stuck in this vicious cycle of heavy, negative feelings for so long you don't know how to get out of it. Maybe you have been told too many times that "you're just sensitive," or "you have an anger issue," or perhaps you've been told, "you have social anxiety."

Hearing labels like this repeatedly may have caused you to believe them. Because you believe them to be true, you might think that this is who you are, and you can't change it.

You are NOT your feelings. Your feelings do not define who you are. In fact, you get to choose how you want to feel in every situation. If you have a feeling you do not want, you have the power to let that feeling go and choose a healthier, more empowering feeling instead.

There are many times that you might have a negative emotion, but that emotion is useful as a learning tool. When you feel that your emotion is useful as a learning tool, you can embrace the moment and decide on a course of action that will bring you the results you want. Often, this too requires you to identify your emotions to focus on the lessons and your desired outcome.

In the case of Beth and Amie, they both decided that their emotions were weighing them down, causing increased tension in their relationship, and are not useful for any purpose. They both want to have a better relationship.

> **REMEMBER:** *You are NOT your feelings. They do not define who you are.*

When you have a feeling you don't want, stop and evaluate it. Once you identify what you're feeling and why you feel that way, as well as if that feeling is useful for any reason, you will have a much more complete picture of what's going on, and you can take charge of your emotion to create the result you want.

CHAPTER FIVE

Question 4:
How Can I See This Differently?

ave you ever made a mistake that you regret and feel
guilty about? The scenario might replay in your head
repeatedly, and you feel terrible about it. The next
thing you know, you are thinking about other mistakes you've
made, and the regret and guilt become heavier and even
overwhelming. It's like watching a train wreck happening
right in front of you and feeling helpless to change the
situation.

Have you also noticed that whatever you focus on grows
bigger and bigger? Focusing on a problem is like feeding it
and giving it the power to grow. If you don't want your
problem to grow, you can choose to focus your energy and
attention on something different. This can be easily
accomplished when you ask yourself, "How can I see this
differently?" When you ask yourself, "How can I see this
differently?" you are actively challenging yourself to find
different ways of looking at the same situation.

It is very easy to answer the question, "How can I see this
differently?" with "I don't know," or "There is no other way

to see this situation differently." I encourage you to use your imagination, be creative, and have fun coming up with different answers. The answers you come up with could be something very appropriate for the situation, or it could be something totally ridiculous that makes you laugh. The idea is to shift your mind away from the negative thoughts and feelings you currently have and into a more positive direction that allows you to take charge of your situation. Remember, whatever you focus your attention on becomes bigger. You have the power to shift your attention away from the problem and toward solutions instead.

Beth realizes that she was not clear in her communication with Amie. She further realizes that her sudden lack of discipline could send Amie the message that she was okay with the new curfew time.

Amie realizes that she has conveniently decided on the new curfew time without clarifying with her mother. Although she still feels her mother overreacted, Amie can see why her mother might feel disrespected and taken advantage of.

REMEMBER: *Whatever you focus on grows bigger and bigger. Focusing on a problem is like feeding it and giving it the power to grow. STOP feeding the things you no longer want and start focusing on what you want instead.*

CHAPTER SIX

Question 5:
Would I Rather Be Right or Happy

A s simple as it may sound, the key to your happiness is simply choosing to be happy instead of fighting, defending, or pushing the other person to accept that you are right.

Choosing to be right gives you only one option. Because you are right, the other person or people are therefore wrong. It is very difficult to be happy with this option because it places the control and power outside of yourself. Since it is someone else's fault, and you can't change the other person, there is nothing you can do other than stew in your negative emotions while being "right."

When you choose to be right, it might seem as if you have won. Even if you "won" the argument, you are probably still not happy because when you force your opinions and thoughts onto someone, you do not restore balance and harmony to the relationship. The negative energy persists.

When you choose to be happy, you open yourself up to options and new possibilities. While you might not be one hundred percent happy with the outcome, you can be happy enough in that moment. That does not mean you have to settle. It just means that for right now, you choose to let go of the negative feeling and focus on a win-win outcome for all involved. When things settle, and emotions are in check, you can calmly bring the topic back up and express your thoughts and feelings in a clear way that helps you get your point across. When you express yourself calmly and clearly, the other person is more likely to hear you out. You are much more likely to get the outcome you are looking for.

Choosing happiness puts the power back into your hands. It allows you to take actions on your behalf, so you can maintain your peace and avoid negative feelings. Choosing happiness allows you to preserve and enhance your relationships while you continue to work toward the best outcome for yourself and those you love.

In the past, both Beth and Amie chose to be right and stood firm on their grounds because both parties saw compromising as "losing." They were both unhappy with the outcome of their continued fights and the increasing rift in their relationship. However, both mother and daughter felt powerless to change because the problem was the other person.

Using the five simple questions as a guide, Beth and Amie decided to let go of their unwanted negative emotions and worked toward understanding each other and rebuilding their relationship.

"Would I rather be right or happy?" is the most powerful question you can ask yourself when you're deciding on what to do with your negative emotion. This question serves as a reminder to choose happiness. In fact, this question is so powerful that you can use it alone most of the time and still get the result you're looking for. If you have difficulty choosing happiness by using this question alone, you can go back and start with questions one through four. By the time you arrive at the fifth question, your mind will be more open and accepting of happiness.

REMEMBER: *When you choose to be happy, you open yourself up to options and new possibilities.*

CHAPTER SEVEN

More Case Studies

L et's look at more scenarios between actual clients of mine and see how they've used the 5 simple questions to reclaim their happiness. In these scenarios, I present only pertinent information as it relates to how these clients used the 5 simple questions. I left non-pertinent information out to avoid confusion and keep these examples brief and on point.

Scenario 1:
Christina and her mother, Amanda.

Seventeen-year-old Christina staggered home drunk after being out all night. When her mother, Amanda, opened the door and saw the condition that Christina was in, she was speechless.

After the initial shock, Amanda started shouting at Christina. Realizing that Christina was too intoxicated for a conversation, Amanda sent her to her room to sleep it off. Amanda planned on speaking to Christina in the morning after she sobered up.

Amanda already caught Christina smelling of alcohol a couple of times that semester. When Amanda asked her about it, Christina brushed it off and said she only tried a sip of beer. She reassured her mother that she was too smart to drink. Amanda felt comforted by the answer and did not push it further. After all, Christina was doing well in school and seemed generally happy.

When Christina came home drunk that night, Amanda was outraged. The outrage continued the next morning as mother and daughter sat down to discuss what had happened. Amanda did her best to stay calm during the conversation.

Christina made little eye contact during the conversation and insisted that she did not understand what the big deal was when "everyone else is doing it."

Christina exclaimed, "I am seventeen and a half, and in six months I will be an adult and can do whatever I want. Why can't you be realistic and just accept that I have the right to make my own decisions?"

Hearing this, Amanda's anger escalated, and she started yelling at Christina non-stop. A thirty-minute lecture ensued, ending with Amanda grounding Christina for a month. In addition, Amanda banned Christina from going out with her friends who were "doing it too." To show Christina how serious she was, Amanda took away her car key and cell phone.

Christina angrily stormed off, threw her lamp across her room, and blasted her music loudly. Amanda was left feeling scared and unsure of how to handle the situation.

Amanda was in a state of disbelief. She was consumed with worries. Questions such as, "What road has my daughter chosen to take? How can she be so irresponsible? What will her life be like if she continues down this path? Where did I go wrong?" flooded Amanda's mind. Images of everything bad that could happen to Christina while she was drunk flashed before Amanda's eyes. The possibilities of Christina hurting herself or someone else brought Amanda to tears.

In the following weeks, Christina tried to get her mother to ease the punishment by attempting to downplay the situation. This worried Amanda even more as she became convinced that Christina did not understand the effects of her actions and the horrific consequences they could have.

With each failed attempt, Christina became angrier and angrier at her mom. Their relationship was becoming worse by the day. Christina became withdrawn, both at home and at school. She refused to talk to her mom, do her chores, or complete her homework. Amanda sought help because she was concerned about Christina's behavior and was uncertain of how to resolve the situation.

Let's see how Christina and Amanda applied the five simple questions to reclaim their happiness and mend their relationship.

Question 1: What Am I Feeling?

When Amanda examines her feelings, she realizes that she feels:

1. Fearful: I'm so afraid that Christina is making a horrible mistake, and this mistake can ruin her life.
2. Overwhelmed: There's just so much negativity, anger, and resentment in the household that I don't know what to do.
3. Guilty: How could I not see the warning signs? I caught her with alcohol on her breath on two

occasions and ignored the problem. She also started making new friends and was more withdrawn this year. Why didn't I see it? Why didn't I intervene?

4. Inept: I'm her mother. I'm responsible for raising her properly. Maybe I didn't do enough for her. She wouldn't be this way if I had paid more attention to her.

5. Powerless: She's so angry with me. We can't even have a conversation. How can I fix this if we can't even talk?

When Christina examines her feelings, she realizes that she feels:

1. Injustice: Mom has such double standards. She drinks with her friends all the time. In fact, just last weekend she came home tipsy.

2. Angry: Mom is so unfair. This is her problem, not mine. I only had a couple of beers. What's the big deal? Other kids my age were drinking so much more. She should be happy I'm responsible enough to stop at two drinks.

3. Frustrated: Can't she see that I'm an adult? I can make my own decisions, and she has to accept that.

4. Defiant: I should just move out on my own. I'm almost eighteen anyway. I don't need this crap.

Question 2: Why Am I Feeling This Way?

Looking at each specific emotion above, Amanda identified several areas of unmet expectations and miscommunications. Amanda realized she expected that her daughter was smart enough to know that underage drinking is illegal and that it is not acceptable in her household. She also expected that, because of her parenting, Christina would adopt the same values and behaviors. Amanda realized that a large part of her fear about Christina's future stemmed from her own bad choices as a teenager.

Miscommunication also played a large part in their problem. Amanda disciplined Christina because she wanted her to understand the seriousness of the situation. Amanda's aim has always been to help her daughter grow up to be a healthy, responsible, and happy adult. Instead of creating a situation for learning and growing, the yelling, threats, and punishment had only caused a deterioration in their relationship, which further escalated the problems.

When Christina stopped and evaluated her emotions, she too found several areas of unmet expectations and miscommunications. First, Christina expected that her mother would not make such a big deal about her getting drunk because Amanda was actually a pretty cool mom who also liked to drink and party with her friends. Maybe a stern lecture, but not grounding her and taking away her social life for a month. Second, Christina felt that since she was almost eighteen, she should be allowed to make her own decisions. She conveniently ignored the fact that it is illegal for her to drink until she is twenty-one years old.

As for miscommunication, the moment she was grounded, Christina got angry and defended her case, rather than taking the time to understand where her mother was coming from. Instead of taking responsibility for her actions, Christina tried to exert her independence and anger by throwing things around and blatantly ignoring Amanda. Christina agreed that her behaviors added to the problem rather than resolving it.

Question 3: Is This Emotion Useful for Any Reason?

Even though both Christina and Amanda agreed that these emotions were useful as a starting point to discuss and resolve their differences, they both realized that there was no point in holding on to the fear, anger, or resentment. They are both willing to work on letting their negative emotions go and creating a happy solution for everyone.

Question 4: How Can I See This Differently?

While Amanda understood that Christina is going through a typical teenage period, where drinking alcohol is starting to be 'cool' for many, the seriousness of that decision still needed to be addressed. Instead of thinking and focusing on all the worst-case scenarios about Christina's life being destroyed, and going into fear and overwhelm, Amanda could have used her energy to come up with effective ways to communicate with her daughter in a way that creates trust while still standing firm to her rules. Amanda could also understand the double standard message she was portraying by coming home tipsy herself.

Amanda reminded Christina that there was a long family history of alcoholism and explained that her fear was largely based on that. In addition, Amanda revealed to Christina some trouble of her own teen years to help Christina understand where her fear came from.

Being reminded of the family history and hearing the stories of Amanda's troubled past helped Christina to understand her mother's reaction and allowed her to feel closer to her mother. Christina finally understood that her mother's fear and reactions came from a place of deep love and concern for her safety and happiness.

In addition, when she examined her own reactions, Christina could see how her actions amplified her mother's concerns and caused a further rift in their relationship.

Question 5: Would I Rather Be Right or Happy?

Having an honest and open conversation helped both mother and daughter release their anger and frustration. Both Amanda and Christina know that there is some work ahead to mend their relationship, but both felt positive and confident knowing that they can put their differences aside and rebuild their relationship.

The Five Simple Questions is a powerful tool to help you understand your emotions, so you can resolve arguments or disagreements in a more positive and productive way—a way that preserves, and even enhances relationships.

Scenario 2:
Amanda vs. Amanda.

Now that you have seen how the five simple questions can be used to resolve arguments with others, let's see how you can use these same five questions to help you release negative feelings you might be holding against yourself.

Let's look at the example above again and see how Amanda used these five simple questions to release her self-judgments.

Amanda realized that besides the negative feelings she held against Christina, she held a significant amount of judgments against herself. These negative self-judgments were clouding her ability to parent, causing her to doubt her efforts, and second guess her actions. This led to poor sleep quality, less energy during the day to focus on her work, and general unhappiness.

To release her self-judgment and reclaim her happiness, Amanda applied the five simple questions to herself.

Question 1: What Am I Feeling?

1. Fearful: I'm so afraid that Christina is making a horrible mistake, and this mistake can ruin her life.
2. Overwhelmed: There's just so much negativity, anger, and resentment in the household that I don't know what to do.
3. Guilty: How could I not see the warning signs? I caught her with alcohol on her breath on two occasions and ignored the problem. She also started making new friends and was more withdrawn this year. Why didn't I see it? Why didn't I intervene?
4. Inept: I'm her mother. I'm responsible for raising her properly. Maybe I didn't do enough for her. She wouldn't be this way if I had paid more attention to her.
5. Powerless: She's so angry with me, we can't even have a conversation. How can I fix this if we can't even talk?

Question 2: Why Do I Feel This Way?

Amanda realized a lot of her negative self-judgments, fear, and guilt were based on the mistakes she had made as a teenager. Amanda didn't realize how much pressure and expectations she had placed on Christina because she didn't want her to make the same mistakes.

Question 3: Is This Emotion Useful for Anything?

Amanda readily saw how harmful it was to hold these judgments against herself. There is no purpose for hanging on to those emotions.

Question 4: How Can I See This Differently?

Amanda realized her self-judgments as being inept and powerless were not true and only served to increase her overwhelm and fear. Amanda has been doing a fantastic job as a mother, sacrificing so much so that Christina could have a great life. Amanda realized that regardless of how she parents, Christina is her own person and will make mistakes as she learns to understand who she is and creates her own value system. Amanda also realized she could improve her parenting and help Christina to make better decisions by explaining the reasons behind her rules, instead of saying "because that's what I expect."

Question 5: Would I Rather Be Right or Happy?

This one was easy for Amanda. She chose happiness for herself and her daughter.

Using the five simple questions, Amanda easily let go of her negative self-judgments, which allowed her to be happier and more productive, both at work and at home.

Scenario 3:
Kelly vs. Kelly

Seventeen-year-old Kelly lost her virginity to an older man she had met at the library a month ago. At first, Kelly ignored Steve's attempts to talk to her. Steve's persistence paid off, and they began chatting when she took a break from her studies. Steve was nice and always made a point to compliment Kelly for both her intelligence and beauty. When Steve asked Kelly for a date, she declined. Steve was much older, and Kelly wasn't sure how sincere he was.

Day after day, Steve would show up at the library just to talk to Kelly. There was never any pressure, just nice friendly chats. After two weeks of this, Kelly decided it was okay to take a walk with him around the lake by the library.

Kelly was surprised by how much fun she had just talking with him. Steve showed genuine interest and care for Kelly. Toward the end of the walk, Steve pulled Kelly close for a kiss. Kelly really enjoyed the kiss and the budding romance between the two of them.

The following week, Steve confessed that he was thinking of her non-stop and has, in fact, fallen in love with her. Kelly was so happy because she knew she had fallen for Steve also. That week, Kelly skipped her library studies so she could go on dates with Steve.

Kelly knew that her parents would disapprove of Steve because of his age, so she kept him a secret from both her parents and her friends. That made the whole romance even more exciting. Steve and Kelly were sharing a secret that only the two of them knew of.

When Steve asked her to skip school the following Monday so they could spend the entire day together, Kelly was elated. She could not think about anything but spending time with Steve. He picked her up promptly at seven-thirty a.m. from her high-school parking lot and brought her to a fancy hotel. He said he wanted to pamper her and give her all the special things she deserved.

That morning, they ordered room service for breakfast, something Kelly has never done before. Steve was so classy and unlike any of the boys Kelly had dated. After breakfast, they went to the beach and picked seashells and played in the water.

After lunch, they went back to the hotel to snuggle up and watch a movie. The cuddling turned into intense kissing and ended up with Kelly agreeing to have sex with Steve. The day was so perfect in every way; Kelly never wanted it to end.

When Steve took Kelly back to school, he kissed her gently and said he couldn't wait to see her at the library again tomorrow. Steve also asked Kelly to think about how she would like to spend their next date together.

Kelly was on cloud nine for the rest of the day. She replayed the beautiful details of their romantic day and lovemaking over and over in her mind.

The next day, Kelly couldn't concentrate on her classes. She continued to fantasize about their next date and couldn't wait to tell Steve about what she wanted to do.

Kelly excitedly ran up the library steps right after school. She knew Steve would be right at the entrance waiting for her just like he had for the past three weeks. When she got to the entrance, Steve wasn't there. Kelly waited and waited. After two hours and endless texts, Steve was still nowhere to be found. Kelly was beside herself with worry but knew she had to go home.

This scene repeated itself for the rest of the week. Kelly would anxiously text Steve every chance she had. To her dismay, there was no answer. Kelly realized that she got so swept up in the secrecy of their romance that she didn't know any of his friends nor where he lived. Kelly felt so helpless. She didn't know what to do or who she could talk to. She was certain that something bad had happened to her love. She contemplated talking to her mother and asking for her help, but the fear of getting in trouble stopped her.

That Friday, as Kelly was sitting at her usual spot in the library waiting for Steve, she overheard a girl talking to her friend about an older man she had met earlier last week. Between tears, the girl told her friend about how this older man had tricked her into sex by sweeping her off her feet. Her description of the man and his actions matched Steve to a tee. Even the term of affection that Steve had called her, "doll face" was the same.

Kelly's heart sank, and she knew she too had been duped by this man. She ran out of the library in tears. Kelly was in a state of shock. She realized she had been used. She had foolishly trusted a man she barely knew. Kelly was angry at herself for being so stupid and naïve. She did not know what to do or whom to turn to. Talking to her parents was out of the question—she dreaded the consequences of her parents finding out she had lost her virginity. She dreaded the consequences of her actions even more. Lost in the special romantic moment, Kelly had agreed to unprotected sex. The possibilities of pregnancy and sexually transmitted diseases frightened her.

For the next few weeks, all Kelly could do was cry and sleep. Kelly's parents tried to talk to her, but she would not tell them anything. Luckily, Kelly agreed to talk to a professional, and her parents brought her in for help.

Kelly was reluctant to share much at first. After much reassurance, Kelly opened up and shared what had happened. She recalled that her shock quickly turned into sadness, which quickly turned into anger. She was angry at him for tricking her and angry at herself for being stupid.

Kelly didn't think she would be willing or able to let go of her anger. In fact, she was scared to let go of her anger because she was afraid that she would be duped again if she let her guard down. After some reassurance, Kelly was willing to use the five simple questions to help her be happy again.

Question 1: What Am I Feeling?

When Kelly examined her feelings, she reports feeling angry (at herself and Steve), disappointed, and fearful of the consequences.

Question 2: Why Am I Feeling This Way?

Kelly identified all three causes of upset as the reasons for her feeling of anger, disappointment, and fear. The first and biggest reason was unmet expectations. She had fully trusted Steve and expected that he was honest and true to his words. She had expected that they were a couple who deeply cared about each other and that the lovemaking was a natural aspect of sharing that love.

As for miscommunication, Steve had purposefully led Kelly on and manipulated her. However, Kelly acknowledged that she made a lot of assumptions based on his actions. Not once did they have a talk about being exclusive or real future plans. Kelly realized she had romanticized a lot and created a romance that was, in fact, amplified by her constant daydreaming.

Thwarted intentions also came into play for Kelly. Kelly had fully intended on carrying on this forbidden romance and had come up with several scenarios of how they could make this relationship work. His lies and deceit thwarted her intentions of a happily-ever-after.

Question 3: Is This Emotion Useful for Any Reason?

At first, Kelly truly believed that holding on to the anger, disappointment, and fear would help her learn her lesson and prevent her from making the same mistake in the future. After examining the situation further, Kelly realized she was only torturing herself by hanging on to these emotions. She realized she had already learned her lesson and felt certain she would not repeat the same mistake. These negative emotions then only served to hold her back and rob her of her confidence and joy.

Question 4: How Can I See This Differently?

Kelly had to come to terms with the situation. Instead of continuing to beat herself up, Kelly decided to accept that she made a mistake for trusting someone she hardly knew. However, that mistake did not make her naïve or stupid. The fact was, this older man preyed on young girls. He was so kind and attentive that it was hard to know he was insincere. Kelly agreed that blaming herself and holding onto the anger and disappointment would only prevent her from healing and moving forward.

Additionally, Kelly could see the potential danger of keeping this to herself. Although Kelly knew it would upset her parents, she also knew just how much they loved her. Kelly needed her parents' support and guidance now more than ever. After all, she had unprotected sex with a stranger who was likely having unprotected sex with other girls. Kelly needed to take care of her physical health as well as her emotional health. At the end of the session, Kelly agreed to share the whole story with her parents.

Rather than continuing to see her parents as a source of potential problems, Kelly decided to see her parents as true allies.

Question 5: Would I Rather Be Right or Happy?

Kelly decided that there was no point in beating herself up any longer. Yes, she had fallen for his tricks, but the man was a master manipulator. Kelly decided that it was time to let go of the anger and disappointment toward herself and embraced the situation as a powerful learning lesson.

Kelly decided to forgive herself and focus her energy and attention back on things that bring her joy.

After talking with her parents, Kelly felt even closer to them than before. One great thing about this horrible situation is that it helped Kelly to remember just how much her parents love and support her.

Once Kelly decided to release her negative emotions and focus on her happiness, Kelly and her parents sought medical care and notified the police about Steve and his predatory actions. Kelly was reluctant to talk to the police at first because she did not much information on Steve and was afraid they wouldn't believe her. However, the officers she spoke with were very understanding and reassured her they would do everything they could to locate and charge Steve. Taking these steps put the power back into Kelly's hands and helped her let go of her fear and move forward.

CHAPTER EIGHT

Get Ready to Reclaim Your Happiness

A re you ready to use the five simple questions to reclaim your happiness? You can use the next few pages to work through some challenges you're dealing with, so you can resolve them in a positive way.

EXERCISE: Think of a recent fight or disagreement you had that you still hold a significant amount of negative feelings about. Remember, this is for you so answer the following questions honestly for yourself. To maximize your results, be creative as you answer the questions. Challenge yourself by putting yourself in the other person's shoes and see things from their perspective.

Write down all the important details of the disagreement.

Question 1: What Am I Feeling?

For this exercise, it is important for you to focus on your feelings rather than your thoughts. The word "think" and "feel" are often used interchangeably, yet, there is an important distinction between them. A thought is defined by the Merriam-Webster dictionary as, "an idea or opinion produced by thinking or occurring suddenly in the mind." Whereas, a feeling is defined as, "an emotional state or reaction." Therefore, a thought refers to a mental process, and a feeling refers to an emotional process.

We frequently use vague terms to describe our feelings, and we commonly mistake thoughts for feelings; our true feelings are often not recognized. Thus, feelings tend to hide below the surface, tucked away so deeply in the subconscious part of your mind that even you are not aware of them. If you don't resolve your feelings, they will continue to hide in the background and affect how you think and act.

Here's an example to demonstrate why differentiating a feeling from a thought is important. Let's say you have a strong feeling of fear when it comes to snakes. Normally, when you think of snakes, you think, "snakes are so disgusting. It makes me sick to my stomach to even think about them." Today, you want to change that, so you changed your thoughts to, "Snakes are okay. I can think about them. It's no big deal." Well, that's a great attitude, but the moment you think about the snakes slithering near you, or thrusting their tongue out at you, you recoil in fear, your stomach turns, and you think, "This is not working. Snakes are disgusting."

If you changed your feeling from fear to neutral, your reactions would be different. When you feel neutral about snakes, you might have unpleasant thoughts about snakes here and there, but you can readily shake it off.

Since "feel" and "think" are often used interchangeably, how can you identify which you are dealing with?

Remember, feelings are emotional states. Examples of feelings you might experience are angry, sad, disappointed, scared, frustrated, stressed, lonely, rejected, or anxious.

Here are examples of thoughts you might have that sound like feelings:

- I feel she lied to me.
- I feel she was wrong.
- I feel that nothing would change, so why bother?
- I feel like I don't know how to fix this.

None of the previous four examples above reflect an emotional state. These are all mental processes.

One way to check to see if you're dealing with a feeling is to replace the word "feel" with the word "think." If the new sentence with the word "think" makes sense, chances are, you're dealing with a thought. If the new sentence makes little sense, it's likely that you're dealing with a feeling.

Let's look at a few examples.

"I feel I'm a disappointment to others," becomes, "I think I'm a disappointment to others." The new sentence makes sense, so it's likely a thought.

Here's another example of a thought that sounds like a feeling. "I feel that no one likes me." When you replace "feel" with "think" the new sentence becomes, "I think that no one likes me." Again, this sentence makes sense, so you're dealing with another thought.

Let's look at a true feeling statement, "I feel sad." When you replace "feel" with "think" you get, "I think sad." The new sentence doesn't make much sense, so the original sentence does, in fact, express a feeling.

When you realize you are dealing with a thought, how do you go further to discover the feeling behind it? To find your feeling, ask yourself, "and that makes me feel ___?" after each sentence you identified as a thought.

In the example above, "I think that no one likes me," you can add, "and that makes me feel _____." Let's say your answer is, "and that makes me feel lonely." Let's check this sentence to see if it is a feeling or thought.

When you replace "feel" with "think" you get, "I think lonely." This new sentence makes little sense. Therefore, you are dealing with a feeling.

Let's say your answer was "and that makes me feel that I can't trust anyone." Replacing "feel" with "think" you get, "and that makes me think I can't trust anyone." The new sentence makes sense, so you're dealing with another thought.

Keep asking yourself, "and that makes me feel_____?" and analyzing it until you identify your feeling.

Another easy way to make sure you are dealing with a feeling is to complete the sentence, "I feel" with just one emotional word. You can go back to the word list in chapter two and pick a word or several words from the list that best describe your current emotional state.

> **EXERCISE:** *Write down all the emotions you are feeling. Remember to be as specific as you can. Rather than staying with the generic, "I feel bad." Work on identifying your true feelings such as, "I feel hurt. I feel annoyed. I feel discouraged." You can also chapter two and identify your specific emotions from the list presented.*

Next, replace "feel" with "think" to see if you are truly dealing with a feeling. (You can skip this if you identified your emotions using the word list provided in chapter two.)

Question 2: Why Do I Feel This Way?

When you use this question with the intention of reclaiming your happiness, focus on identifying which of the three causes of upset you're dealing with, instead of justifying your emotions. Remember, all three of the causes might be involved. Here's a quick reminder of the three causes of upset feelings:

1. Unmet expectations
2. Thwarted intentions: something that stops or keeps you from what you've intended to do or to make happen
3. A miscommunication or misunderstanding that leads to #1 or #2 above

If you need a more detailed reminder of what the three causes of upset feelings are and why it's important to identify them, you can go back and review chapter three.

Here's an example of justifying your feelings. "I'm angry because she didn't return my sweater even though I asked for it three times."

Instead, you can say, "I'm angry because when I loaned her the sweater, I asked her to agree to return it to me on Friday. She did not meet the expectation that we had set."

> **EXERCISE:** List your feelings and the reasons for them by filling in the blanks.
>
> *I feel* _____ *because* _____.

Question 3: Is This Emotion Useful for Anything?

Initially, many people will say, "Yes, my negative emotion is useful," and they will say something similar to:

*   I need to make the other person pay.

- I don't want to look weak.
- If I forgive them, they will do it again or think I'm stupid.
- I don't want to make the same mistake again.
- They hurt me so badly, and I can't just let it go.

In reality, holding onto negative emotions only hurts you. Think about it. When you hold onto your negative emotions, it feels heavy and burdensome. It makes it hard for you to think about something else or enjoy yourself. Do you really want to give someone else the power to control your happiness?

Forgiveness doesn't mean that you agree with what they did. Forgiveness means taking your power back and saying, "I am strong enough to let this go so I can be free to focus on what's important to me."

> **EXERCISE:** *Ask yourself, is this emotion useful for any reason? If you answer yes, write down how it helps you. Then go back and review what you wrote and see if that is really the case. Does holding onto those negative feelings really free you and allow you to do the things you truly want to do.*

Question 4: How Can I See This Differently?

You already know how you feel about the situation so use your imagination to come up with creative ways to see the situation differently. Here are several ways to help you change your perspective quickly and easily.

1. For a moment, put yourself into the other person's shoes and see things from their perspective. Ask yourself, "What could be going on in this person's life that is causing them to think, feel, or react this way?"

2. If that's too hard to do, pick a person or even a made-up character that you admire, and imagine how they would see the situation. For example, "How would my dad think or feel about this situation?" or "How would Superman think or feel about this situation?"

3. You can also pretend you're watching a movie and the situation was a scene from that movie. How would you see that situation differently then?

4. Perhaps you can pretend that your very best friend or the person you love most just experienced your exact scenario. How would they view the situation? What would they do differently?

EXERCISE: Use your imagination to create three different versions of how you can see this situation differently.

Question 5: Would I Rather Be Right or Happy?

This question is hard for many people when they first read it because they think they are happy when they are right. There are many occasions where you are right and happy. However, when you're dealing with a negative emotion such as anger or disappointment, choosing to be right and holding onto your emotion also means that you give up your real happiness.

Think about it. When you choose to be right and hold on to your negative emotions, are you truly happy? Did you and the other person make-up and you both feel good about the outcome or do you still feel a sense of tension or disconnection between you and the other person?

Remember, being happy doesn't mean you have it your way. It means that you choose to put the differences aside or to let go of your negative emotions so you can focus on creating what you truly want instead.

> **EXERCISE:** *Ask yourself, am I ready to give up feeling _____ so I can be happy instead?*
>
> *If you answered, yes, the next chapter could help you reclaim your happiness.*
>
> *If you answered no, ask yourself, what am I afraid would happen if I stopped feeling _____. Then go back and answer questions one to five again.*

You deserve to be happy, and happiness is simply a choice! Whenever possible, choose happiness for yourself!

You might be wondering, "Okay, I have decided to be happy, but I don't feel any better. Now what? How can I actually let things go and move forward?"

Deciding to be happy is a crucial step to being happy. Once you've decided to be happy, then you can begin to take action to be happy. In section four, we will discuss three techniques you can use to reclaim your happiness.

CHAPTER NINE

How to be Happy

What if you did, in fact, choose to be happy, but you are still having a hard time letting go? What can you do?

One way to be happy is to focus your attention and energy on doing something you really enjoy. This tells your mind that even though things aren't going the way you want them to go, you are still the one in control of your feelings and you can choose to do what makes you happy.

This is not the same as pretending that you are not bothered and mope. This is actively choosing to do what you love and feeding that positive energy to help it grow.

REMEMBER: What you focus on grows bigger and bigger. Rather than focusing on the problem, focus on something you enjoy and let that good feeling grow.

Reclaim Your Happiness Option 1:

Write down as many things as you can think of that you enjoy doing that are fun or relaxing to you. Think of things that you can do that make you smile, laugh, or fill you with motivation, happiness, or positivity.

Here are some examples:

I enjoy watching funny cat videos, listening to music, reading a book, working out, going to the beach, talking to my friends, playing video games, dancing, and hiking.

> **EXERCISE:** *Make a list of things you enjoy doing. Come up with as many as you can think of. When you want to reclaim your happiness, look at this list, pick out one or two things, and do the things you enjoy.*
>
> *Keep adding to this list as you find more things that bring you happiness.*

Reclaim Your Happiness Option 2:

Another option is to be fully present with your problem. Start by recognizing and accepting that things aren't the way you want it to be. However, instead of sulking and allowing your emotions to control you, take charge. Ask yourself, "What would I like to see happen and what are one or two things I can do right now to move in that direction?" This puts the power back in your hands as you focus your energy on working toward a solution instead of feeling helpless or like a victim.

When you don't like your current situation, and you want to be happy, you can choose to focus on the solutions instead of the problem.

The first step is to decide how you would like to see this situation resolved. It would be nice if the situation got fixed or changed to your exact liking, but chances are, that might not happen right away. So instead, focus on your short- term goals.

> **EXERCISE:** *Ask yourself, "What can I be happy enough with right now, knowing that this is only a beginning step toward my ultimate goal?" Next, ask yourself, "What are one or two things I can do right now to move toward my desired outcome?"*

Reclaim Your Happiness Option 3:

Another way you can create happiness and focus on the solutions is to use the "Start, Stop, and Continue" method.

First, you want to identify your short-term goals. Ask yourself, "What can I choose to be happy enough with right now, knowing that this is only a beginning step toward my ultimate goal?"

Second, ask yourself, "What could I choose to START doing to help me achieve my goals?"

Third, ask yourself, "What could I choose to STOP doing that would help me to achieve my goals?"

Fourth, ask yourself, "What could I choose to CONTINUE doing to help me achieve my goals?"

For example, let's say you and your mom have been fighting because she feels that you are not taking your schoolwork seriously. Let's also say that you are taking your schoolwork seriously, but you are struggling with math and you don't want to admit it, or don't know how to ask for help. Your mom is frustrated that your grade is slipping. You're trying your best, but you just don't get math and your mom's constant nagging weighs heavily on you, making it even harder to focus on your schoolwork.

Using the Start, Stop, and Continue method, you might create a plan that looks something like this: (Just jot down ideas or phrases. They don't have to be complete sentences.)

1. Short-term goal: bring my grade up from a C to a B in one month
2. START:
    - Ask the teacher for extra help and extra credit assignments
    - Talk to Mom about getting a tutor
    - Partner with other students to work together
3. STOP:
    - Stop procrastinating
    - Stop spacing out when things make little sense during the lecture
    - Stop pretending that I don't care about my grades
4. CONTINUE:
    - To do my best
    - To complete all assignments on time
    - To stay committed to my education

EXERCISE: *Identify your goals and your START, STOP, and CONTINUE plan.*

Step 1: What are my short-term goals?

Step 2: What could I choose to START doing?

Step 3: What could I choose to STOP doing?

Step 4: What could I choose to CONTINUE doing?

Once you've created your happiness plan, regardless of which option you choose, the next step is to follow through. Take small, consistent steps daily, and you will start creating a healthier, happier outlook and positive habits for yourself. Like anything else, with practice, you'll find that it gets much easier to focus on positive solutions rather than hanging on to the bad feelings.

You now have some very simple yet effective tools that put the control and power back in your hands. What you do with this is up to you. I hope you recognize just how much power you have over your emotions. Things that used to bother you in the past don't have to bother you anymore because you can let them go. Remember, you deserve to be happy!

I would, but
MY DAMN MIND
won't let me!

A Guide for Teen Girls:
How to Understand and Control Your Thoughts and
Feelings

Book 2 of 3 from the

Words of Wisdom for Teens Series

Jacqui Letran

DUNEDIN, FLORIDA

Table of Contents

Book Two: I would, but MY DAMN MIND won't let me!

CHAPTER ONE

Why Can't You Just Control Yourself?

How many times have you been told by well-meaning parents, adults, or even your friends that you should just stop thinking or feeling a certain way? They tell you that the problems you have are all in your head. They tell you to stop making a big deal out of things, that you're too sensitive, and there is no reason to be nervous or anxious.

And yet, you are. You don't know what to think or how to feel. You feel tense and nervous. Others seem to have it so easy. But for you, life is difficult and so unfair!

Your situation may seem hopeless; perhaps you have even concluded that you were just "born that way" and there is nothing you can do to change.

But what if you are wrong about that conclusion? What if there was a way for you to create the changes you desperately desire? What if I can teach you how to take control of your mind, thoughts, and feelings? Would you want to learn how to do that for yourself?

The power of the human mind is incredible. It is capable of creating horrible life experiences, and it is capable of creating happy, successful ones, too. It might not feel that way right now, but you do get to choose which life experiences you'll have.

Once you learn easy, yet highly effective ways to take charge of your mind, you'll find that you have the power to create the life you want and deserve. The power to create permanent, positive change is available to you no matter what you are struggling with.

Stop wasting your energy and time on those old, useless emotions and thoughts. Today is the day to change your life experiences.

This book will show you how to:

- Challenge your old negative belief patterns.
- Stop unhealthy thoughts and feelings.
- Create positive life experiences for yourself.
- Stay calm and in control in any situation.
- Unleash the power of your mind to create the life you want and deserve!

Everyone's journey to happiness begins with the belief that happiness is possible. Even if your personal experiences have led you to believe you will have a difficult life filled with stress, anxiety, and unhappiness, I will show you that you do have other options. You can learn to believe that happiness is possible for you.

In this book, I will show you how to take charge of your mind to overcome your obstacles and struggles. I will show you simple, yet powerful principles to strengthen your self-belief that leads to a solid foundation for happiness and success.

The next time somebody asks you, "Why can't you just control yourself?" you can smile and thank them for the gentle reminder and instantly take control of your thoughts and feelings again.

You are the key to your success and happiness.

Close your eyes and imagine for a moment how wonderful your life will be once you fully understand how to control your thoughts, feelings, and actions. If you are ready to make that dreamlife your reality, I encourage you to read this book with an open mind and a willingness to try something new.

Get ready to be amazed at how quickly you can take charge of your life now.

60-Second Reader

1. You get to choose which life experiences you'll have.
2. You have the power to create the life you want and deserve.
3. The power to create permanent positive change is available to you, no matter what you are struggling with.
4. You can learn to:
   - Challenge your old negative belief patterns.
   - Stop unhealthy thoughts and feelings.
   - Create positive life experiences for yourself.
   - Stay calm and in control in any situation.
   - Unleash the power of your mind to create the life you want and deserve.
   - You can learn to be happy.

Self-Reflection

Take five minutes to think about how your life will be once you can stop those negative thoughts from occurring and instead, focus on the positives of every situation. What would that look like? What would you do? How would your life be different?

Use your imagination and have fun with this self-reflection. Write down all the wonderful things you'll finally be able to do. Remember to dream big!

CHAPTER TWO

Your Conscious Vs.
Your Subconscious Mind

To take control of your mind, it is important to understand the differences between the conscious and the subconscious mind and the roles that each part of your mind plays in your life.

Your Conscious Mind

The conscious part of your mind is your logical self. It can see the past, present, and future. It solves problems and stores your goals and dreams. It has free will to reject or accept concepts and ideas.

There are three main things to know and remember about your conscious mind:

1. It's responsible for logic, reasoning, and decision-making.
2. It controls all of your intentional actions.
3. It acts as a filtering system, rejecting or accepting information.

What Does This Mean?

The conscious part of your mind is the part that you are aware of. It's the part of your mind that you use when you are learning a new concept. For example, it helps you to learn how to ride a bike. When you are in the learning phase, you are consciously focused on how to balance yourself, how to pedal, how to move forward without crashing into something or losing your balance. All those thoughts and actions are the work of your conscious mind—something you are fully aware of.

Your conscious mind is also responsible for collecting data, processing the data, and making decisions based on the data at hand. It is the part of your mind that makes simple decisions such as, "I want to wear that black sweater because it looks good with my jeans." It also makes more complicated decisions, such as what college to apply to base on the career path you desire.

While your conscious mind is amazing in its ability to collect, process, and make sense of the data, it has its limitations. Did you know that your conscious mind can only process less than one percent of all the data available to you at any moment?

At any given time, you can only consciously focus on less than one percent of all the things that are going on within yourself and your environment.

Even if you could process ten times this amount, you would still be missing ninety percent of the facts and data available to you. That's an incomplete picture if you ask me.

Knowing that now should cause you to ask some questions about your life experiences so far: "What have I been missing? What information did I not even detect? How would my life be different if I have access to different information?"

Later, I will explain this concept and show you how to use this knowledge to take control of your thoughts and actions so you can take control of your life. Before we dive into that, let's talk about your subconscious mind and its functions.

Your Subconscious Mind

Your subconscious mind reacts based on instincts, habits, and learning from past experiences that are programmed into what I call "the Master Plan."

The Master Plan is a detailed set of instructions (like a movie script) that tells your subconscious mind what to do. Your subconscious mind does not have free will. Any ideas, thoughts, or feelings that get into the subconscious part of your mind stay there.

There are five main things to know and remember about your subconscious mind:

1. It is responsible for all of your involuntary actions (breathing, heartbeat, etc.).
2. It is one hundred percent automatic and follows scripts; it has no ideas and thoughts of its own.
3. It stores ALL of your memories, life experiences, learned information, and beliefs.
4. Its main function is to keep you alive and "safe."

5. Your subconscious mind processes information through pictures and images (or what is call an "Internal Representation," or "IR" for short).

REMEMBER: *The subconscious mind is that part of your mind that is NOT within your awareness. It works quietly behind the scenes, tucked away in a dark corner, so no one will notice it or its activities.*

Unlike the conscious part of your mind that can only process up to one percent of the available data, your subconscious mind can process one hundred percent of every bit of data it encounters, every second! That's right… your subconscious mind is one hundred percent aware of everything that's happening within you and around you, every single second of every single day.

The Master Plan

When you were born, you were born with a "pre-programmed" Master Plan, which is a detailed set of instructions and algorithms that tells your subconscious mind what to do. In your infancy and early years, that Master Plan includes only rudimentary, yet very important instructions that tell your subconscious mind what to do to keep you alive—such as breathing or regulating your heartbeat.

This Master Plan also has information handed down from your parents and ancestors in the form of genetics, such as your hair and eye color.

However, you were not born with the Master Plan for your belief system, core values, or the things you will learn in the future. Most of the information you'll need to create the majority of this Master Plan will be given to you during the first seven years of your life by those who interact with regularly, and through your own life experiences.

Your Master Plan is ever-changing, a constant work in progress. It is always adapting and evolving based upon your current situation and the aspirations you have for yourself.

Your conscious mind is responsible for adding to the Master Plan based on your life experiences. In a future chapter, we will discuss how your conscious mind programs the Master Plan. For right now, just know that there is a Master Plan from which your subconscious mind operates.

Your Subconscious Mind Simplified

To simplify the concept and help you understand the power of your mind, I want you to think of your subconscious mind as nothing more than a room full of movies—a movie library of your very own. In your movie library are hundreds of thousands (or even millions!) of movies starring you and your life experiences.

Within this movie library, there is a recording device and a Movie Operator. Your Movie Operator's job is to follow the Master Plan, which is a pre-programmed set of detailed instructions and algorithms provided by your conscious mind. In this way, your conscious mind is like the writer and director, and your subconscious mind is the actor or actress carrying out the directions within the scripts.

The recording device within your subconscious mind is always "on" and actively recording everything you are experiencing, every second of every day. Every one of your experiences EVER—whether it's a thought, a feeling, or an action—are recorded as a movie.

Using the instructions in your Master Plan, your Movie Operator labels, sorts, and stores your movies into your subconscious mind's library. That Master Plan also tells your Movie Operator when to store or remove a movie from your "favorite playlist" and when to play a movie back to you.

Besides recording, sorting, storing, and playing your movies, your Movie Operator has a bigger job. That job is to protect you and keep you safe from any real or perceived danger. Similar to the first job, your conscious mind has also created a Master Plan of what to do in every potential situation. That's an enormous job, but the only tools your subconscious mind has are the movies it has recorded of you and the instructions in the Master Plan.

Who's the Boss?

Given the information presented so far, who do you think is the boss—your conscious mind or your subconscious mind?

If you choose your conscious mind, you are correct!

Your conscious mind is always the boss. It's the part of your mind capable of processing and analyzing data. It's the part of your mind that has free will to make decisions and can accept and reject information. It's the part of your mind that filters information to come up with the Master Plan.

Your Reality Exists Only in Your Mind

Do you remember when I said your conscious mind can only process less than one percent and your subconscious mind can process one hundred percent of the data you encounter? What does that mean?

To put things into perspective, your subconscious mind receives millions of bits of data every single second. Millions of bits of data every single second! Stop and take that in for a moment. Every single second of your life, your subconscious mind is bombarded with millions of bits of data, which is equivalent to all the words in seven volumes of average-sized books. That's a lot of information to process every single second.

Imagine what it would be like for you if you were aware of millions of bits of data every single second of your life. How would you feel if you were forced to process seven volumes of books every single second? Your conscious mind is just not capable of processing that much data. You would go into severe sensory overload and would most likely explode or shut down. Luckily for you, all of that is happening in the background of your subconscious mind and is not within your awareness.

Of the millions of bits of data, the conscious part of your mind can only process 126 bits of data per second. To show what this looks like, let's look back at the example of the millions of bits of data as being equivalent to all the words within seven volumes of books. Of the seven books that your subconscious mind is processing, your conscious mind can only see one word. One word! That one word, whichever one word that might be, is the only one that makes it into your awareness and becomes your reality.

I want you to stop and think about what that means. Imagine reading seven books and understanding only one word, thus believing that one word is, in fact, the only subject of those books. Is there something you might be missing?

The important takeaway here is to realize that each of us is most likely focusing on a different word that becomes our respective realities.

REMEMBER: *Your reality only exists in your mind and nowhere else. You might have a similar experience to that of another person, but when you break it down into tiny details, you will find significant variations.*

Try this exercise out for fun. Close your eyes and turn to a random page in this book and point to a word. Now, open your eyes and look at that word. Does this one word represent everything this book is about?

I can guarantee that the answer is no. This book is much more than the one word you've randomly picked, but that shows how your conscious reality might be twisted by the powerful filtering system of your mind.

The Importance Center

How does your mind decide which one word out of the seven volumes of books to focus your attention on? Within your mind, you have a part called the Reticular Activating System.

The Reticular Activating System is responsible for many functions. In this book, I will focus on its role in creating your reality. I like to refer to the Reticular Activating System as the "Importance Center," or "IC" for short.

Remember when I mentioned the Master Plan before? The Master Plan is kept here in the IC and tells your subconscious mind what information to send to your conscious mind.

All of your significant information is stored here—your belief systems, your values, your significant emotional experiences, and your significant learning situations.

REMEMBER: *Your Importance Center is as unique as your fingerprint. No two people have the exact same Importance Center. That is why you can be at the same event as someone else and have a completely different experience.*

From the millions of bits of data it receives, your subconscious mind filters them through the IC. If it matches the content within your IC, that information gets delivered to your conscious awareness. If it doesn't match the content within the IC, your subconscious mind will either delete it, generalize it, or distort it to make it "fit" in with your Master Plan.

Let's say your mom bought a brand-new car—a white Honda Accord. Soon after, you begin to see the same vehicle in the same color as your mom's car everywhere you go. Did a bunch of people suddenly buy the same car as your mom?

No. Most likely, those cars have been on the road all along, but it wasn't an important detail for you until your mom bought the car. Once your mom made that purchase, the details of the car entered your IC and instruct your subconscious mind to bring it into your awareness.

You might be hyper-aware of white Honda Accords for a while, but once the car becomes old news, you stop seeing them nearly as much. Does this mean that tons of people sold their car, and they are off the road? No. All it means is that, at this moment in your life, the Honda Accord is no longer of significant importance, so it doesn't get delivered to your conscious mind at every sighting.

It's important to note that the IC has short-term and long-term parameters or instructions that it's following. Short-term parameters are things that might be important to you right now, for a brief time—similar to what's in style right now or the newness of a song. It could be a few days, a few weeks, or even months, but short-term parameters have an end date.

Long-term parameters stay with you for long periods of time. Often, they stay with you permanently unless you purposefully remove those parameters. Long-term parameters can be as simple as learned activities such as riding your bike or more complex, such as your belief systems.

The Personal Assistant
You Didn't Know You Have

How would you like to have a personal assistant who is there for you 24/7? How amazing would it be to have not only such an assistant but one who eagerly awaits your every command and obeys those commands without questioning you? That sounds amazing, right?

What if I told you that you actually do have that personal assistant already, but you have been giving your assistant bad commands? Commands that are getting you the results you are experiencing right now. Results that you may no longer want. Would you want to learn more about your assistant and, more importantly, learn how to command your assistant to create the results you want?

You might have guessed by now that your subconscious mind is your personal assistant. Your subconscious mind's job is to deliver to you whatever experience you are looking for in the easiest and quickest way possible.

What you might not know is that every thought you have and every feeling you feel is a command to your subconscious mind to give you more of the same.

That's right. Every thought you have and every feeling you feel is a command to your subconscious mind, "This is what I want. Give me more!"

If you said, "I'm so stressed," your subconscious mind heard that as a command: "I want to be stressed. Look for evidence to support why I should be stressed. Give me more reasons to feel stressed."

Once you give that command, your subconscious mind will immediately look for stressful details in your environment. Details that could stress you out get pushed to your IC and into your awareness. In addition, your subconscious mind will also look in your movie library to find your stressful movies to play in the background for you. You are the boss. When you ask for stress, your subconscious mind is happy to deliver it to you.

Does this sound familiar? How many times have you felt stressed out about something, then started having stressful thoughts about something else and soon, you were overwhelmed with stress and other negative feelings? This is because whatever you focus on grows bigger.

REMEMBER: *Whatever you are focusing on, you are telling your subconscious mind to give you more of that thing. It's like feeding a monster food and watching it grow out-of-control right in front of your own eyes.*

The good news is that the process works both ways. This means that when you focus on something positive, that positive thing will also grow. If you are stressed out, you can focus on being calm instead.

Choosing Calm

You have an assistant who will obey your every command, so use your assistant to your benefit. In stressful moments, you can say to yourself, "Even though I feel stressed, I choose to be calm."

Say, "I choose to be calm" several times to catch your assistant's attention. After saying that three times, start repeating, "I am calm. I am calm. I am calm," repeatedly. As you repeat, "I am calm," imagine yourself doing something that calms you down. It might be reading a book, laying out on the beach, or taking a nice, soothing bath.

With these steps, you are telling your assistant, "Even though I am stressed, I choose to be calm. Calm looks like this. Go get it for me. Give me more of this." It makes it simple for your subconscious mind to bring you to calmness.

Regardless of what negative emotion you experience, I recommend that you give your assistant the command to bring you calmness. Calmness is a wonderful place to be. Being calm is like a reset; it shuts down the old negative movies, so you have a blank screen. From a place of calmness, it is easier to look at the current situation for what it is and make decisions that best suit your needs.

REMEMBER: *Whether you focus on the negative or the positive aspects of any event, you have to spend energy on those thoughts. Why not focus your energy on positive, powerful thoughts that will create the results you're looking for?*

What Does Google Have to Do With Your Mind?

Here's another detail that is important to command your subconscious mind effectively. Your subconscious mind is like a Google search engine. Whatever you type into the search bar, when you press "enter," you'll get results that match that search request.

Just like the Google search engine, your subconscious mind cannot process negative commands. When you give your subconscious mind a negative command, it will ignore the negative part of it and focus on the remaining part of the command.

This is because of the Internal Representation (or IR) that I mentioned in the very beginning when we talked about the subconscious mind.

Remember when I said that your subconscious mind processes information by creating pictures and movies? When I say, "Think of spilling milk," what picture came to mind for you? That is how your subconscious mind understands those words.

If I say, "Don't spill the milk," what picture comes to mind? You can't form a picture of "Don't spill the milk." What might pop up instead is a picture of you holding onto a cup or glass carefully or something similar. That is not the same as "Don't spill the milk." Your subconscious mind, like the Google search engine, cannot process negatives. It cannot make an IR of a "don't" or a "not."

With Google, if you type into the search bar, "Don't find me blue shoes," and press "enter," Google will deliver you tons of things related to blue shoes. It completely ignores the "don't" part.

Try it out for yourself. Do a Google search using "don't" and see what results you'll get. Better yet, let's do a simple experiment right now. Ready? Here it is. My command to you is, "Don't think of an orange elephant."

What happened? The first thing you thought of was an orange elephant, wasn't it? When you realized you were thinking of an orange elephant, you might try to force yourself to think of the elephant in a different color or think of something else entirely different. That's interesting, isn't it?

You should have some "aha" moments right now. Think back over the past week or two and consider what commands you have been giving to your subconscious mind that are causing you to have some of your negative feelings and experiences.

Now that you are aware of how your subconscious mind interprets instructions, be very aware of the thoughts you're thinking and the feelings you are feeling. If the thoughts or feelings are negative, you can choose differently instead. This is where the "I choose to be calm" instruction comes in handy. That thought lets your assistant know you have chosen to be calm instead of upset or stressed, or whatever you may have been feeling.

REMEMBER: You are the boss, and your subconscious mind is your assistant. If you catch yourself giving your subconscious mind a negative thought or bad command, do something about it. Your assistant will carry out whatever command you provide unless you consciously revise it.

Let's say your mom is making dinner. She asked if you would rather have chicken or fish. You said fish but immediately changed your mind to chicken. When you realized this, chances are you corrected yourself and told your mom you wanted chicken. I doubt that you would just sit there and expect she would read your mind and prepare chicken instead.

You could do the same thing with your subconscious mind. Let's say you thought, "I'm too angry to focus now," and you catch yourself thinking that. Rather than just letting it go, you can say, "Whoops, I mean I'm willing to focus." Or you can say, "Erase or delete that," or similar phrases to tell your subconscious mind what you want to do with the misinformation. You can also say, "I'm in control of what I focus on."

The "I choose to be calm" command works fantastic here, too. Commands like these are very powerful because they tell your subconscious mind exactly what you want.

60-Second Reader

1. Your conscious mind is your logical mind that learns, thinks, and decides.
   a. You use this part of your mind to focus on details and become aware of things.
   b. You can only consciously focus on one percent of what's happening inside of you and around you at any given moment.
2. Your subconscious mind is like a program, running automatically in the background of your mind.
   a. You do not have an awareness of, nor can you focus on the automatic programs of your subconscious mind.
   b. Your subconscious mind can process one hundred percent of everything happening inside and immediately around you.
3. Your "Importance Center," or "IC," contains the automatic programs of your subconscious mind.
   a. Your beliefs and other significant information are stored in your IC.
   b. Your subconscious mind is programmed to look for evidence to support whatever is in your IC.
   c. Your IC is unique to you. No one else has the exact same IC as you, which also means no one else experiences things the way you do.
4. Your subconscious mind is your Personal Assistant, and you are the Boss.
   a. It's programmed to give you the experiences you ask for in the easiest, quickest way possible.

     b.   Problem: Every thought you have and feeling you feel is a command to your subconscious mind, "This is what I want; give me more!"

5. Your mind is like a Google search engine. It cannot process negative commands.

     a.   When you give a negative command, such as "Don't be angry," your subconscious mind will ignore the "don't" and will carry out the rest of the command.

     b.   Solution: Give your mind clear, positive commands of what you truly want. Instead of saying, "I don't want to be angry," you can say, "I choose to be calm."

CHAPTER THREE

The Belief System

B elief:

1. An acceptance that a statement is true or that something exists.
2. Something one accepts as true or real; a firmly held opinion or conviction.

Did you know that most of your belief systems were developed by the time you're seven years old? Did you also know that most of your belief systems were not decided by you but, in fact, were given to you by someone else?

I want you to stop and let that sink in for a bit. Most of your belief systems about who you are and the world around you were given to you from birth to the age of seven.

Why birth to seven years old? During this part of your growth and development, your subconscious mind is fully formed and operational. However, your conscious mind, the logical part of your mind, is just beginning to form and is not fully working yet. This is why little kids believe in everything they see or hear. The Easter Bunny, Santa Claus, and the Tooth Fairy are all one hundred percent real to your younger self because your conscious mind is not developed enough to say "No, that's not true."

The Creation of Beliefs

There are five main ways for you to develop a new belief:

1. Evidence: This is a rational decision based on cause and effect. For example, every time you break curfew, you get grounded. You will create a belief that breaking curfew results in being grounded.

2. Tradition: This is based on your family and cultural values. For example, you're raised in a Catholic family, your belief system will carry many facets of the Catholic teachings.

3. Authority: This is based on what the people in respected roles teach you or tell you about something. An example would be your doctor diagnosed you with depression; therefore, you believe you have depression.

4. Association: This is based on the people you interact with. For example, if you belong to the Mensa Club and interact with a bunch of intellectuals, you might believe that intelligence is valued.

5. Revelation: This is based on your gut feelings, insights, and intuitions. For example, sometimes you just have that gut feeling of "I don't trust this person," although you might not know why.

Your subconscious mind records one hundred percent of everything, but that doesn't mean everything you experience becomes part of your belief system. In the beginning, when you do not have a Master Plan for new ideas or a belief system yet, your subconscious mind just records your events. It doesn't have a label for those events yet, nor is there a way for it to sort and categorize them.

Everything your subconscious mind records at this point is stored in a "general" category. In fact, in your mind's movie library are many categories of beliefs, similar to "genres" or "types" of movies. The four main movie types are:

1. Instructional: These are things you've learned to do such as riding a bike or playing the guitar.
2. Factual: These are things you've learned to accept as truth, like different colors or your date of birth.
3. Emotional: These are the experiences you've had and what the experiences mean to you specifically.
4. General: This is where all the miscellaneous movies are stored.

Let's look closely at how an instructional movie might get made. Imagine you are an eight-month-old infant learning how to use a spoon. If you have seen a baby learning how to use a spoon, you know how messy that process is. Often, the baby is shoveling food onto her chin or cheeks or drops it onto herself completely. That is because there is no instructional tape in her subconscious mind's library that tells her how to feed herself properly yet.

The first time you tried to feed yourself, your subconscious mind records the event and stores that movie in the general category of your movie library. The second time you attempted to feed yourself, your subconscious mind records it and stores it in the general category again. The third time you tried to feed yourself, your conscious mind might recognize the same data pattern and tell your subconscious mind to sort and store them together.

Once you fully know how to use a spoon to feed yourself, it becomes an instructional video for "Feeding Self with a Spoon." The next time you go to feed yourself, your subconscious mind replays that movie in the background, and you feed yourself easily without thinking about it.

Consciously, a lot of things were happening simultaneously for your subconscious mind to sort and categorize that movie. Perhaps your mom said, "Let's learn how to use a spoon today" or something similar every time she handed you a spoon. With repetition, you consciously learn that when your mom says, "Let's learn how to use a spoon today," and hands you an object; that object is called a spoon, and it is used to put food in your mouth. You then use this information to create your instructional video.

Major belief systems are created similarly, either through a single significant emotional event or repetitions of several low-intensity emotional events.

Significant Emotional Events

Imagine that you are three years old and you're playing in your room. Like most three-year-olds, you are making a huge mess, throwing things around, and having a great time. Your mom comes into the room, sees the mess, and gets furious with you. She might force you to quit playing and clean your room. She might yell at you or, if you're in an abusive situation, you might get hit on the head or kicked or something similar.

This is definitely a significant emotional event for your three-year-old self. You were just having fun in your room when suddenly your mom grabbed your toys away, hit you on the back of your head, and yelled, "You're a bad girl. Clean up your room now!" You don't have a full understanding of what just happened. All you know is that your fun ended, your mom is angry, and you are in pain. Because this event was so traumatic and the pain was significant, your conscious mind immediately accepts this to be a fact and creates one or more beliefs about this event.

Some beliefs that might develop from this incident are:

1. Having fun is bad. When I have fun, I get punished.
2. I am a bad girl. I made Mom angry.
3. I am helpless. There is nothing I can do to fix this.
4. I am not loved.

These and other potential beliefs become a part of your Master Plan with instructions and strategies on how to avoid these painful events.

Your subconscious mind recorded the whole event, labeled it, and filed it under all the applicable beliefs. Because there are instructions in the Master Plan about this event, this movie gets placed into the IC immediately. Your subconscious mind is now programmed to look for evidence of these beliefs and to bring matching details to your conscious awareness immediately.

Repetitive Low-Intensity Emotional Events

Imagine again that you are a three-year-old, playing in your room and making a huge mess. Your mom came into the room, saw the mess, and said in a soft but stern voice, "Look at this mess. You're a bad girl." Your mom might take your toy away, or she might make you clean it up. You were having fun, and she interrupted it.

The emotions attached to this event are low in intensity. You might be upset, but it wasn't a significant emotional event. Still, your subconscious mind recorded it and filed this movie away in the general category of your movie library.

If this happened repeatedly, it becomes a different story. Let's say the exact scenario happened again three days later. Your subconscious mind makes the same recording and filed it away with the first recording. At this point, these videos are not important yet. However, let's say it happened again two to three more times. Your conscious mind might create these beliefs:

1. Having fun is bad. When I have fun, I get punished.
2. I am a bad girl. I make Mom unhappy.
3. I am helpless. I want to play, but Mom won't let me.

Similar to the significant emotional event example, if this happened repeatedly, your conscious mind would include this data in the Master Plan, thus telling your subconscious mind to look for evidence to support these belief systems.

Remember, beliefs are created whenever you have a significant emotional event or if something keeps happening repeatedly.

Here, Take This Belief and Make It Yours

Earlier, I said that most of your beliefs were given to you. How is that possible and why is that the case?

From birth to seven years old, your conscious mind is not fully formed or fully functional yet. If you hear something repeatedly, especially if it's from someone you love or who has authority over you, you will believe what they say is the truth.

For example, if you grew up in a poor household and heard your parents fight about money constantly or heard them say things like, "It is so hard to make money," or "Those greedy rich people," you might create a belief system of:

1. Money causes people to fight.
2. It's hard to make money.
3. Rich people are greedy.

Similarly, if you grew up with a man-hating angry mother who constantly said, "You can't trust men," "All men are pigs," or "All men are controlling," you would also believe these generalities to be true about men.

Remember, low-intensity repetitive events and significant emotional events create beliefs.

Sleuthing for Evidence

Let's pretend that the incident with the three-year-old I mentioned above happened to you and now, you have a belief of "I am a bad person." Once a recording is placed into the IC, your mind is being directed to look for evidence to support that belief system for the rest of your life.

You carry your belief system with you wherever you go. It's like carrying a basket around with you for the rest of your life to look for evidence to put into it. If a friend, uncle, or aunt says, "You're a bad person," you'll pick this information up and put it into your basket to validate your belief system. Same with any comments from anyone else that matches the belief system.

Soon enough, you are carrying a basket full of evidence to support why you are such a bad person. It feels heavy, burdensome, and overwhelming to have to carry this extra weight everywhere you go. You become tired and you have no energy or motivation to do the things you want to.

Because you have a belief system of "I'm a bad person" in your IC, your subconscious mind will only shift data that matches that belief system into your awareness. If someone said, "You are such an amazing person," you either don't hear them at all, or you hear them, but don't believe it. In fact, you might even try to prove that the other person is wrong.

A good example of this is to think of a time when someone has given you a simple compliment that made you feel uncomfortable. How did you respond? You might have said nothing because you didn't know how to react since you don't believe what they've said. You might have deflected that compliment, given credit to someone else, or downplayed it completely because you were uncomfortable. You may even interpret their words as sarcasm or false flattery.

Changing Beliefs

Although most of your belief systems were developed between birth to seven years old, you can create new belief systems after seven.

Any time you experience a significant emotional event once or a low-intensity emotional event repeatedly, you can create new belief systems. You can also develop new belief systems when you, on purpose, decide you want to change.

Some beliefs are easy to change because they are in your awareness. When your belief is within your awareness, you can decide what you want to do with it. Deeply buried beliefs are much harder to change. Even then, changing your subconscious belief system is definitely possible. It requires working with someone knowledgeable on how to help you access the contents of your subconscious mind and deliver them to your conscious awareness in a safe and gentle way.

60-Second Reader

1. Most of your belief systems were developed from birth to seven years old.

    a. Your conscious mind, the logical part of your mind, is just beginning to form and is not fully working until around the time you turn seven.

    b. This is why little kids believe everything they see or hear.

2. Beliefs are created whenever:

    a. You have a significant emotional event.

    b. Something happens frequently.

3. Once you create a belief, it goes into your IC and your subconscious mind is programmed to look for evidence to support it.

4. Although most of your belief systems were developed between birth and seven years old, you can create new belief systems after seven.

    a. Any time you experience a significant emotional event once or a low-intensity emotional event repeatedly, you can create new belief systems.

    b. You can also develop new beliefs when you, on purpose, decide you want to change.

CHAPTER FOUR

The Stranger Danger Protocol

How many times have you been told that in order for you to accomplish something, all you have to do is use your willpower? And how many times have you tried using your willpower, and yet, you did not achieve your goals?

You might have been frustrated or disappointed with yourself. You might even become angry with yourself. You might even believe that you are a failure.

Willpower doesn't work if your subconscious belief systems do not align with your goal.

It is very common for people to start a goal with excitement and determination, then give up on it soon after. This is because their conscious desires do not match the subconscious beliefs they have programmed into their Master Plan.

Let's use a common scenario to illustrate this. Pretend you want to lose ten pounds. You read a news article that inspired you. It says if you eat under thirteen hundred calories daily and exercise three times per week for thirty minutes each time, you'll lose ten pounds in two weeks.

You think, "Wow! All I have to do is keep my caloric intake to less than thirteen hundred calories per day and exercise thirty minutes a day, three times a week; I'll lose ten pounds in two weeks! It seems simple enough, plus it's only two weeks! I can do this!" You set on your weight loss path with determination and even perhaps some excitement.

Soon after you started this new healthy program, something changed that inevitably stops you from moving forward in achieving your goals. That something is your subconscious mind, and it screams, "Change is scary; change is dangerous."

Remember earlier, I said your subconscious mind's primary aim is to keep you safe? Well, safe doesn't mean "safe" according to your subconscious mind.

Your subconscious mind is programmed to accept that "safe" means "DO NOT CHANGE. CHANGE IS SCARY. CHANGE IS DANGEROUS! STAY EXACTLY AS YOU ARE RIGHT NOW!"

Whenever you attempt to make a change that disrupts the status quo of your current belief system, your subconscious mind freaks out. It assumes that you are in danger and it will do everything it can to get you back to its perceived safety.

Let's look at the weight loss example again. For the sake of this example, pretend you are three hundred pounds and everyone in your family weighs three hundred pounds. Also imagine you have been struggling to lose weight all your life.

Imagine reading an article that motivates and inspires you to take actions to lose weight again. You're excited! This is the thing that will finally help you lose weight! This is your answer!

When you decided to follow the new program, that was a conscious decision. As you do the prescribed activities, you feel good about yourself. You feel hopeful because you are still within the safety zone according to your subconscious mind. As you move away from the safety zone and into a new territory, or "the danger zone," your subconscious mind freaks out and thinks you're in danger. Since its job is to keep you safe, it will do all that it can to get you back to its perceived safety zone. It activates the "Stranger Danger Protocol."

REMEMBER: *The purpose of the Stranger Danger Protocol is to make you doubt yourself, put you in a place of fear, or make you feel bad by reliving past failures, so YOU STOP what you're doing and go back to where it feels safe again.*

To get you to stop your new activities, your subconscious mind might play your old movies that cause you to doubt yourself. Movies that make you think, "Can I do this?"

"What would make me think this would even work?"

"I've tried so many things, and nothing worked!"

"It's genetic and there's nothing I can do about it."

Or it might play fearful movies. "It will be so hard to exercise three times a week. It will aggravate my left knee again!" Or perhaps, "It will be so boring eating nothing but fish and vegetables. I can't even be social; everyone I know only eats burgers and fries!"

Perhaps your subconscious mind might play movies of your past failures. Maybe you've lost five pounds in the past only to gain ten pounds back. It will replay those old movies, causing you to re-experience the old pain of failure.

Not only are the old painful movies playing in the background, but your subconscious mind will actively scan your environment looking for evidence to show you why you will fail.

If you are like most people, when you have doubts, fears, or you remember your past failures, you will stop doing those new activities and go back to your old ways. It seems too scary or even pointless to try.

Every time you start and stop like this, you strengthen your "I can't" belief system. Soon, the belief system becomes so heavy and so powerful that all you have to do is think about your goal and you'll go into an anxious state.

The Root of Most Problems

The Stranger Danger Protocol is not the only tool your subconscious mind has to keep you from changing. In your subconscious mind's library catalog are the four main themes I've mentioned, Instructional, Factual, Emotional, and General.

Within the Emotional Category are four main subcategories:

1. I'm Not Good Enough.
2. I'm Not Worthy.
3. I'm Not Loved.
4. I'm Not Safe.

We all have these four main subcategories in our IC. It is part of our Master Plan, created by us, to keep ourselves safe. It is also the root of most problems that we, as humans, encounter. How many movies you have in each of these subcategories depends on you, your beliefs, and your life experiences.

The details of your movies differ from other people because your movies are based on your specific life experiences and belief systems. However, regardless of who you are, these four main subcategories are there in varying degrees, hidden in a dark corner, ready to unleash at any moment.

In the next few chapters, I will discuss each of these belief systems further. But right now, let's imagine one of your big belief systems or emotional subcategories is, "I'm Not Good Enough." Because this is a significant belief system, it is housed in your IC and your subconscious mind is programmed to constantly look for evidence to support this. No matter where you are, no matter what you are doing, no matter who you're with, your subconscious mind is constantly looking for evidence to support that you're not good enough.

Imagine in the background of your mind is a movie playing on a repetitive loop, 24/7, of all the instances that prove you're not good enough. This movie plays on and on, getting louder and louder as you attempt to do anything that might threaten or contradict this belief system.

Imagine that 24/7, you are receiving messages of "You're not good enough." These constant negative thoughts and feelings keep you stuck. The fear and doubts that often go hand-in-hand with these messages prevent you from taking actions and moving forward because it seems too scary or pointless to fight a losing battle.

Most of the time, you are unaware of the movies your subconscious mind is playing in the background for you. However, as you continue to challenge any significant belief system, the applicable movies get louder and more vivid; you might even get a conscious awareness of bits of it. However, most of the time, you are not fully aware of the exact cause of your underlying belief system. You might have a feeling of fear, anxiety, or discomfort that you can't fully explain.

Taming Your Subconscious Mind

What do you do when you want to change an underlying belief? How can you change your behaviors and belief systems when your subconscious mind is fighting you every step of the way?

The first step is to recognize that you are the boss, and your subconscious mind is only following the instructions you have programmed into your Master Plan. Because you are the boss and you are the one responsible for programming the Master Plan, you can also change the Master Plan.

To begin, you want to acknowledge your negative emotions and decide you want to make a change. Next, create small, simple goals for yourself. In the case of the ten-pound weight loss, your small, simple goal might be to lose just one pound. Then, perhaps step it up to three pounds, then five pounds, eight pounds, and finally, ten pounds.

When you first start on this journey, you'll feel good because you're doing what you consciously wanted to do, and you are within your safety zone. Soon after, you will enter the perceived danger zone and your subconscious mind will start freaking out. It will reach for and play your old, negative movies again.

However, this time, your goal is small and simple. You push through the slight discomfort to reach your first small and simple goal. Once you reach your first goal, your subconscious mind cannot deny that you have met the goal. To keep your subconscious mind stable, you do whatever you need to do to maintain the one-pound weight loss.

Do not attempt to lose any more weight at this point. You hang out at your new weight for a while to allow your subconscious mind to realize that you are "safe" and that this is your new normal. From that new starting point, you push again until you reach the next goal. As before, when you reach your next goal, you just hang out there for a little while to allow your subconscious mind to establish this as a new safety zone.

How long you have to hang out depends on the belief system you are challenging, how long that belief system has been around, and the emotional charges attached to it. You will know it is time to work on the next small, simple goal when you feel comfortable, and it is effortless to maintain your current achievement.

You might be wondering, "If my conscious mind is the boss, why can't I just change the Master Plan at will? Why do I need to make these small, simple goals?"

Your conscious mind is, in fact, the boss and you can, in fact, change the parameters within the Master Plan. You can change the details within your Master Plan easily when the belief is within your awareness and is of low emotional intensity.

However, when you experience something with significant negative emotions, you learn that it is too painful, and you don't want to experience that emotion again. To make sure you never experience that pain again, when you program your Master Plan around that experience, you put up as many booby traps as you can to protect the Master Plan. This is why you have to take small, simple steps to diffuse the booby traps without setting off the alarm.

If you take these small, simple steps in real life, it might take years to accomplish your goals depending on what they are. I know you don't want to wait years to achieve your goals. You want to achieve your goals now, or at least in a relatively short amount of time.

The cool thing is that there are simpler, more effective ways to achieve these goals quickly. For one, you can speed up the process significantly by vividly seeing yourself completing your goals and completing them well repeatedly. This works because your subconscious mind is constantly creating movies for you.

The good news is that your subconscious mind can't tell the difference between a real event you're experiencing versus something you are vividly imagining. To your subconscious mind, it is the same. It records, sorts, and stores them both the same way.

You can use this information to your advantage. Let's say you have a goal to be comfortable and confident in doing a class presentation. Vividly see yourself standing up in front of the classroom, feeling good about yourself and feeling confident that you know your material well. Vividly see yourself presenting with a strong and assured voice, making great eye contact and feeling at ease. Vividly imagine yourself completing the presentation and answering questions with authority and confidence.

As you imagine these scenarios, bring in as much detail as you can. Use all of your senses. See it. Touch it. Hear it. Taste it. Smell it. Feel the emotions attached to it. The more details that you provide, the better your recording will be and the quicker the change will occur.

Sports stars have been using this technique for centuries with amazing results! A tennis star, for example, might vividly imagine himself performing a perfect serve repeatedly—perhaps twenty times before a match. When he steps onto the court for his first serve, his mind thinks it is the twenty-first serve. His mind is calm and focused. His body is relaxed. He carries out his serve with confidence and power. This simple little technique can help you achieve any goal in your life easier and quicker.

While this technique is very useful in helping you achieve many of your goals, other goals are harder to achieve with this method alone, especially if they are deeply rooted in your belief systems. For example, if your father regularly beats you from the time you were an infant to the time he left when you were nine years old, it might seem almost impossible to forgive him. You can definitely use the visualization technique mentioned above and achieve your goals, but that could take significant effort and dedication because of all the booby traps you have laid around this belief system.

In instances of deep-rooted, especially traumatic beliefs, it is best to involve the guidance of a highly trained professional who specializes in addressing the subconscious mind. They can help you identify your troubling belief system, the source of its creation, and the negative emotions attached to them.

Once the negative emotions are identified and released, the belief becomes neutralized; you are then free to reprogram that part of the Master Plan.

REMEMBER: *When your conscious and subconscious minds are in conflict, your subconscious mind always wins.*

To be successful in creating your desired changes, you must resolve your issues at the root of the problem—that means addressing your subconscious mind. Failing to do so will cause you to revisit that problem repeatedly. The most effective therapies for changing deep-rooted belief systems address the subconscious mind directly.

In the coming chapters, I will share stories of some real-life clients of mine who resolved their problems quickly once they understood how to address their subconscious mind. I will share their main emotional subcategory and how it showed up in their lives. See if you can relate with one or more of them to begin your own self-discovery.

60-Second Reader

1. Willpower doesn't work if the goal you want to achieve is not aligned with your subconscious belief systems.

2. Your subconscious mind's primary aim is to keep you safe.

    a. Safe doesn't mean "safe" according to your subconscious mind.

    b. To your subconscious mind, change is scary. Change is dangerous.

    c. Whenever you attempt to change something that disrupts your current belief system, your subconscious mind freaks out. It thinks you're in danger and it will do everything it can to get you back to your "safe" place.

3. Your subconscious mind uses the Stranger Danger Protocol to get you back to your "safe" spot.

    a. The Stranger Danger Protocol will make you doubt yourself, make you fearful, or make you feel bad by reliving past failures, so YOU STOP what you're doing and go back to where it feels "safe" again.

4. Most problems can be traced back to one or more of four faulty beliefs:

    a. I'm not enough.

    b. I'm not worthy.

    c. I'm not loved.

    d. I'm not safe.

5. To tame your subconscious mind, start by being the Boss of your mind. Give your subconscious mind clear and direct commands.

    a.   Create small, simple goals that lead to the ultimate big goal to prevent the Stranger Danger Protocol from being activated.

6.   Your subconscious mind does not know the difference between what's real and what's imagined. To your subconscious mind, it's the same.

    a.   Whatever you want to achieve, vividly imagine yourself already achieving that goal. Be sure to attach strong, positive emotions as you imagine your achievements to help your subconscious mind quickly accept it as "safe."

    b.   This simple little technique can help you achieve any goal in your life easier and quicker.

7.   When your conscious and subconscious minds are in conflict, your subconscious mind always wins.

CHAPTER FIVE

I'm Not Good Enough

I'm not good enough is the biggest, darkest emotional subcategory in your movie library. At the root of most problems is an underlying belief that you're not good enough.

Before you dismiss this notion as a possibility, know this belief is often hidden under the surface of your conscious thinking and can still be a significant source of trouble for you.

This belief system might show up as:

- I'm not [insert your word here] enough (i.e., smart, tall, beautiful, funny, old).
- I can't seem to do anything right.
- Others are always doing better than I am.
- I have nothing important to contribute.
- There is something wrong with me.
- I'm not good at anything.

Study: Stressed-Out Samantha

Client: Samantha, Age 15½

Presenting Problem

Samantha had been becoming more withdrawn over the past few months. Her mother is concerned because she suddenly lost 20 pounds, has no appetite, and is having difficulty keeping up in school. Samantha used to be a straight "A" student, but now she is struggling to keep passing grades. Currently, she is at-risk for failing one class because she is behind on several writing assignments. She is also getting a "C" in another class.

Samantha reports feeling overwhelmed by the ever-increasing stress and responsibilities. She has a difficult time saying "no" and, as a result, she does whatever people ask of her. She takes on too many tasks and then feels burdened by the commitments. As a result of feeling overwhelmed, Samantha has a difficult time focusing during the day and sleeping at night. Simple tasks are now difficult.

Family History

Samantha's parents were divorced when she was eight years old. She currently lives with her mom and two younger brothers. She describes the relationship between her mom, siblings, and herself as being pretty good. For a while, she was seeing her dad every month since the divorce. That relationship is described as extremely stressful because "I could never make him happy." In fact, it's so stressful that she hasn't seen or spoken to her father for close to a year. He rarely attempts to contact her.

Social History

Samantha is shy and has a few close friends. She used to enjoy hanging out with them, but lately, she finds it hard to enjoy herself socially. Samantha reports having difficulty opening up to people, even to her close friends.

Words Samantha Often Heard Others Used to Describe Her

Smart, studious, giving, nice, mature, responsible, generous

Words Samantha Uses to Describe Herself

People pleaser, weak, can't say "no," invisible, and pushover

Session One Notes

Growing up with her father was difficult for Samantha. Her parents fought constantly. There were many screaming and yelling bouts between her parents. Whenever her parents would fight, her father would belittle Samantha. He would be demanding, verbally abusive, and always had to be right. He was cold and distant.

Samantha can't recall her father ever saying, "I love you," or "I'm proud of you." When she tried to hug him, she was mostly pushed aside or told to go play somewhere else.

From a very early age, Samantha tried everything she could think of to get her father to like her. She would play quietly when he was around. She tried to do her best in school and even played sports that she didn't care for, just because her father liked the sport. Occasionally, her effort would pay off and her dad would give her some attention.

While Samantha was not completely aware, the theme for Samantha going through life was, "I'm not good enough."

Root Cause

We traced back to an incident when Samantha was five years old. After a horrendous fight between her parents, Samantha decided to draw a picture for her father to cheer him up. Samantha spent a long time perfecting it; drawing and erasing, redrawing and erasing until she thought it was perfect. When she was finally satisfied with her work, she excitedly approached her father. With a big smile on her face, Samantha presented her artwork and said, "I drew this picture for you, Daddy. I hope this makes you happy."

Her father looked over at her briefly and didn't say a word or make any attempt to reach out to receive his gift. Samantha stood silently and held her breath for what seemed like hours to her. Still, there was no response from her father. Slowly, Samantha approached him with his gift stretched out in front of her. Her father grabbed it, looked at it, and said, "You think this is going to make everything better? Look at it. It's so sloppy. There's nothing good about this picture!" He then crumpled up the drawing, threw it in the corner, and went back to ignoring Samantha.

Samantha stood there motionless, too scared to cry or move.

In that very moment, Samantha recalls feeling:

1. Angry: How can he be so mean? Even if he didn't like it, he doesn't have to treat me that way.

2. Confused: Why didn't he like it? I spent so much time and energy on it. I thought it was pretty and that it would make him happy.

3. Self-doubt: Do I even know what pretty is? Am I sloppy? I can't seem to do anything right. What's wrong with me?

4. Fear: His anger is always so scary to me. He is so cold. I can never tell what he will do next.

5. Sad: My father doesn't love me. I'm unlovable.

6. Helpless: I can't change the situation. There's nothing I can do.

7. Self-hate: I'm no good. I can't do anything right. I can't make my dad happy.

As Samantha recalled the story, she felt significant anger toward her father. She couldn't understand how someone could be so cruel. Samantha now recognized how this single significant emotional event resulted in her pattern of trying to please everyone as an attempt to feel valued and loved.

After working on releasing the anger, Samantha revisited the memory with a new perspective. She recognized that her father was unhealthy, and his actions reflected the way he felt about himself. Samantha finally understood it was not about her at all. She was just a convenient and easy target for his anger. She decided to forgive her dad.

Samantha could not believe how much of a burden it was to seek her father's approval continuously. She felt liberated and excited to learn to be the source of her own "approval machine," as she called it.

Three-Month Follow-Up

Samantha has reconnected with her father. She finally told him how much his actions had hurt her. She also told him she forgave him. Samantha reports being very surprised when her father became teary and hugged her. Her father even apologized and promised to do better. It was a wonderful day for Samantha.

Samantha Also Reported

1. She is all caught up in her classes and is passing all of them.
2. She feels good about herself.
3. She sleeps better now and is more focused when she is at school.
4. She is more aware of her own needs and can say "no" to activities that do not interest or suit her.
5. She feels more confident in who she is and what she is capable of.

Six-Month Follow-Up

Samantha's relationship with her father is still distant. He did make some minor efforts to tell her he is happy with her occasionally. However, he still acts cold and is often aloof. Samantha now realizes that her father is not mentally healthy and no longer takes his actions as a personal attack or a reflection of who she is.

Samantha reports that she is going out with her friends so much more. She feels comfortable and at ease when she is out. Something that surprised her is that she feels much more adventurous than she ever thought she would.

Lesson Learned

Samantha had always wanted to please people. She did not understand why she felt that way. Even when she was overwhelmed, she still couldn't say "no." This was because of that significant emotional event she had experienced at age five that caused her to believe she wasn't good enough for her dad. She felt unlovable, so she continued to do everything she could to earn his love.

Occasionally, her efforts paid off and her father gave her the attention she had been craving. This reinforced to Samantha that to be loved, she must do everything she could to prove that she is good enough and worthy of love.

Once she neutralized the emotions attached to this incident, she could see the situation for what it was and realized the error of this belief system. The problem wasn't that she was not good enough; the problem was that her father was not emotionally healthy enough to show Samantha love in a warm or consistent manner.

Realizing this allowed Samantha to consciously change her beliefs and recognize her true self-worth. She no longer needs validation from others to feel good about herself.

REMEMBER: There are always more sides to the story than just your side and things are most often not what they seem at first.

When things are not going well for you, rather than focusing on what's wrong and making the problem bigger, ask yourself, "How else can I see this situation differently?"

Have fun with this question. Be a detective and look for clues that point to the possibilities of different conclusions, happier conclusions.

When you have a strong negative reaction to something, you can bet that there is an underlying belief at play. Be willing to pause, examine the situation, and identify the potential negative beliefs, or "trigger," for your feelings. Be willing to let go of your original thought or belief and become open to seeing evidence of the new (and improved) conclusions you've just created. You might just find yourself pleasantly surprised.

Self-Reflection

1. What is your biggest take-away from this chapter?
2. How can you use what you've just learned to take charge of your mind and be a happier, more confident you?

CHAPTER SIX

I'm Not Worthy

Many times, the "I'm not good enough" and "I'm not worthy" beliefs go hand-in-hand. It often looks like this, "I don't deserve _____ because I'm not _____."

This belief system might show up as:

- I don't deserve to be successful because I'm lazy.
- I don't deserve this award because I'm not smart.

"I'm not worthy" can also result from having guilty feelings because of something you have done in the past.

Case Study: Miserable Megan

Client: Megan, Age 18

<u>Presenting Problem</u>

Megan sought help because she was recently diagnosed with depression and was prescribed Zoloft and weekly counseling. Megan attended nine sessions and stopped going because she did not notice any improvement. She also stopped taking her Zoloft due to dizziness, headaches, and stomach pain while she was on it.

Megan reported being "cursed with uncontrollable negative thoughts." No matter what was happening, Megan would play out negative scenarios in her mind. She feels consumed with these negative feelings and thinks she's losing control of her mind. Even when things are going well, Megan reports feeling anxious and fearful that "something bad" was about to happen.

The situation was so bad that Megan had to quit her part-time job at the local movie theater because she was too emotional and cried easily.

Family History

Megan is an only child and reports having had a better-than-average childhood. Her parents were and still are loving and supportive. Her mom and dad often praise her and brag about her to others constantly. Megan recalls hearing her parents say things like, "Megan is so perfect. We are so lucky to have such a wonderful daughter," and "I wouldn't know what to do if we had a problem child," referring to the girl next door.

Social History

Megan reports making friends easily. She has always been one of the popular girls in her school. She volunteers weekly at various local community centers.

Words Megan Often Heard Others Used to Describe Her

Beautiful, smart, funny, giving, generous, friendly, kind

Words Megan Uses to Describe Herself

Fake, phony, a bad person, ugly, unworthy, liar

Session One Notes

Megan was very closed off at first. She hardly made eye contact, preferring to hide her face behind the office pillows. Megan insisted she doesn't know why she feels she is a bad person, but just knows that she is. She consistently said, "I don't deserve to be happy. I've done many bad things and I can't change them." Megan would not discuss what those bad things were, but would say, "The people at work don't like me," and "I hurt people."

Session Three Notes

Megan is more comfortable and is opening up significantly—although cautiously—in each subsequent session. She shared several incidences that "prove" she's a bad person in her own eyes. She also shared a story of something that happened when she was twelve years old—the reason she hates herself so much and believes she is undeserving.

That year, Megan had entered middle school and started attending a new school. Although there were many new students, Megan felt very comfortable in her new environment and, as always, made friends easily. Like previous years, Megan began hanging out with the popular older girls within a few weeks. Life was easy for Megan.

For Megan's friend, Ashley, life was just getting difficult. Ashley had always been small, young looking for her age, and socially awkward. Being around the older girls made it even more obvious just how small and awkward she was. Ashley did not fit in and was an easy target at school.

Megan sobbed loudly as she recalled an incident when some popular girls started teasing Ashley about her awkwardness and size. Ashley began crying and looked over to Megan. "She was begging me to help her with her eyes," Megan cried.

For some unknown reason, Megan felt angry with Ashley for putting her in the middle of this situation. Unsure of what to do, Megan looked away and pretended not to notice the pain and humiliation Ashley had to endure. Although her inner voice said, "Do something!" Megan continued to pretend to be oblivious to Ashley's plight.

Megan cannot recall what happened after that but stated she felt so guilty for what had happened. She has not forgiven herself for being a coward. In fact, Megan admitted that all of her good deeds are just her effort to hide the fact that she was such an ugly and weak person.

Megan was hesitant to forgive herself at first. She was scared that if she let go of the guilt and shame, she would start engaging in those horrible activities again. After reassurance, Megan was willing to start the self-forgiveness process. At the end of that session, Megan reported feeling much better about who she was and what she had done.

Root Cause

Feeling lighter and more hopeful, Megan started working on discovering and eliminating other significant negative emotional events.

Megan was very shocked when a memory of an incident came up from when she was seven years old. Megan and her parents were over visiting at their neighbor's house for dinner one night. Megan and Riley (the neighbor's nine-year-old daughter) were playing in Riley's bedroom while the parents were in the kitchen, preparing dinner.

Megan spotted a pretty pink box and asked Riley to show her what was in it. Riley excitedly pulled out a new necklace her mother had just given her a week before and showed it to Megan with pride. Carefully, Riley put the necklace back into its box before returning to play with Megan.

After dinner, Riley's mother asked Riley to retrieve her new necklace to show Megan and her parents. Riley ran to her room and came back empty-handed.

Riley said the necklace was missing and accused Megan of stealing it. As soon as the accusation left Riley's mouth, her mother yanked her over and started shouting at her. "You lost your new necklace? You are so careless. You don't deserve anything nice. How can you blame little Megan for your carelessness? I'm so disappointed in you!"

Riley tried to defend herself, but her father stepped in and sternly told her to go to her room and "Think about the trouble you are causing for your mother."

Crying quietly, Riley left the room. On her way out, Riley looked at Megan, but Megan avoided her eyes, too ashamed of herself because she knew the truth.

Later that night, Megan went outside to throw the necklace away. Upon entering her house, Megan overheard her mother saying, "I can't believe that Riley. She is such a bad girl, blaming our little Megan like that. Megan is so perfect. I don't know what I would do with a problem child like that."

Megan felt sick to her stomach. She was certain that if her parents knew the truth, they wouldn't love her anymore. That night, Megan cried herself to sleep.

This memory surprised Megan as she hasn't thought about this incident for many years. Recalling it now, Megan felt so much shame and guilt again. She can't believe that she never confessed. In fact, over the next few weeks after that event, Riley had begged her to return the necklace several times. Each time, Megan would look away and say, "I don't know what you're talking about. You're a liar!"

With significant reassurance, Megan was willing to forgive herself and accept that she was just a little girl then, doing the best she knew how at the time, and it is now time to forgive herself and move on.

After several rounds of forgiveness work, Megan reported feeling significant relief. For the first time in many years, Megan finally saw herself as a good and kind person. She recognized that her kind acts were not an act. She truly enjoyed helping people. Megan could finally see herself for the kind and giving young woman she is.

Three-Month Follow-Up

Megan reports feeling happy and free. Megan credited her new outlook on life to her ability to forgive herself. Occasionally, the self-doubts would come back. Each time they came back, Megan overcame them by reaffirming, "I forgive myself. I am a good person. I am worthy of happiness."

Lesson Learned

Guilt is a powerful negative emotion that can hold us back and cause significant pain. In Megan's case, although she had forgotten about the incident with Riley, that incident was a significant emotional event for her that created a lot of negative beliefs.

Once she created the belief that she was a bad person—and therefore, did not deserve to be loved—she unknowingly programmed her mind to look for evidence to support that belief system. Her mind did exactly what she instructed it to do and made her hyper-aware of many incidences that matched this belief system. Many of those incidences were minor, yet still played an important part in validating her beliefs.

Forgiveness is the antidote to guilt. When you forgive yourself, you release the burden of guilt. That doesn't mean that you condone what you did, nor that you think it's okay to repeat the action. When you forgive yourself, you recognize and accept that you did the best that you knew how to do at the time. You give yourself permission to let go of the guilt so you can move forward in peace. From a place of peace, you can make much better decisions for yourself and your future.

REMEMBER: If you are holding guilty feelings about something, now is the right time to let it go. Give yourself permission to release it and forgive yourself. You do not need the guilt to avoid the same mistake or to "learn your lesson." Once you have forgiven yourself, you will become much freer, and your decisions will be clearer.

Self-Reflection

1. What is your biggest take-away from this chapter?
2. How can you use what you've just learned to take charge of your mind and be a happier, more confident you?

CHAPTER SEVEN

I'm Not Loved

A s humans, we all have a strong need to feel loved and be connected to others. Love is such an important emotion that it drives many of our thoughts and actions. When we feel loved and connected, life seems easier somehow. When we lack love and connection, we often feel lonely and incomplete.

"I'm not loved" often shows up as:
- Nobody likes/loves me.
- I'm all alone in this world.
- Everybody abandoned me.
- I'm unlovable. Who would love me?

Case Study: Angry Jessica
Client: Jessica, Age: 16

Presenting Problem

Susan brought her daughter, Jessica, in for help because of Jessica's increasing anger outbursts in the past few months. Within the past three weeks, things have gotten significantly worse, with Jessica getting into two verbal fights and one fistfight at school. Jessica is also fighting with her younger sister daily. Susan feels hopeless and unsure of what to do. The counselor at Jessica's school recommended that she sees her doctor for medication to "calm her nerves."

Family History

Jessica lives with both parents and a younger sister. Jessica has never been close to either parent. Her older brother, Jonathon, was her best friend and idol. A drunk driver killed him when Jessica was nine years old. Her little sister, Jennifer, was born the following year. Jessica has always resented Jennifer.

Social History

Jessica is a good student who excels at math, English, and arts. She is a bit of a loner and has only one close friend and several acquaintances. While she is liked and welcomed by other people, Jessica prefers to be alone. Jessica spends most of her time listening to music and drawing.

Words Jessica Often Heard Others Used to Describe Her

Talented, quiet, artsy, loner, nice, smart

Words Jessica Uses to Describe Herself

Artsy, creative, loner, angry, alone in this world

Session One Notes

Jessica was full of anger and frustration when she came in. She said she hated feeling this way, but she also doesn't know how to stop. She spent the first 15 minutes of the session pacing back and forth while talking to me. After doing a few relaxation exercises, she finally calms down.

Jessica expressed significant anger toward her parents. She feels the only time they paid any attention to her was when she was in trouble; otherwise, they act like she doesn't exist. Jessica hates being a part of her family. "Everyone is messed up, yet they (referring to her parents) always pretend that we're the perfect, happy family."

Jessica spent most of the session venting, rapidly firing off all the "stupid" stuff her parents did to keep their perfect, happy family front.

Her thoughts were racing, and many ideas did not connect. Jessica would break down and cry in frustration because she couldn't express herself.

We spent much of the session practicing calming techniques and allowing Jessica to vent and cry.

Session Two Notes

Jessica was much calmer today. She proudly stated that she has been doing her calming exercises, and they have been helping to take the edge off.

We spent today exploring the death of her brother and what it meant to her.

Jessica recalled that her childhood was great. Although she didn't have a close relationship with her parents, things were OK between them. She received all the love and attention she needed from her brother, Jonathon, who was also her best friend. They did everything together. Even when Jonathon's friends wanted to exclude Jessica, he would always choose her even if meant being excluded himself.

Jonathon was a wonderful artist, naturally. His drawing talents were well known at school. Jessica had always admired that about Jonathon. In the six months preceding his death, Jonathon had taken a significant interest in helping Jessica develop her drawing abilities. They would spend hours creating and perfecting their work.

Then, the nightmare happened. Jessica came home from grocery shopping with her mother to see many flashing lights from police cars in the street by their house. Her mother ran from the car, toward the house, only to be caught by a police officer who held her back. He said something to her that Jessica couldn't hear. Then Jessica heard the loudest, most terrifying scream she has ever heard and watched as her mother fell to the ground, continuing to wail loudly.

Jessica crept in for a closer look. Before another police officer could stop her, Jessica was standing beside her mother. In front of them was her brother's body on a stretcher. Jonathon's shirt was cut down the middle, exposing his chest. A man pulled a blanket up to cover his body and face. Before they fully covered him, Jessica remembered the cold stares from her brother's eyes—an image that still haunts her today. A drunk driver had hit and killed Jonathon as he was riding his bike in front of their home. Jonathon was 13 years old.

That night, family and friends gathered at the house to grieve and to give Jessica's family support. Although the house was filled with people, Jessica had never felt more alone than that night. Nothing was real to her. Everything and everyone moved in slow motion. Intellectually, she knew her brother had passed away. Emotionally, she couldn't accept it.

At one point that night, Jessica shouted at everyone to stop crying and go home. She didn't want to play this stupid game anymore. Jonathon had to be alive. Jessica ran around the house calling out for him to stop hiding and come out.

Jessica was quickly ushered to another room by her aunt. "You need to be brave and strong for your parents. You need to put on a brave face. They cannot deal with any more pain right now," she said and hugged Jessica.

For the rest of the night, Jessica sat quietly by herself, holding onto her drawing book for dear life. That was her only connection to Jonathon.

That night, Jessica was told to sleep in the living room so that her aunt and uncle could sleep in her room. Being in the living room by herself was so scary for Jessica. It was so big and cold. Jessica was all alone as everyone was upstairs.

Lying in the dark, Jessica felt:

1. Lonely: There is no one here for her.
2. Confused: Why did her brother have to die?
3. Unloved: There is no one left to love her.
4. Abandoned: How could her brother leave her?
5. Scared: Who will protect her now?
6. Burdened: She had to put on a brave face for her parents.
7. Sad: Her best friend is gone.
8. Fear: She couldn't get the memory of her brother's cold eyes out of her mind.

Jessica was surprised at how much detail she remembered and how much pain she still carried. With help, Jessica released most of the pain she had experienced that night.

Session Three and Four Notes

The first few weeks after Jonathon's death were unbearable for her. Not only did she lose her brother and best friend, it felt as if she also lost her parents as well. Her mother never left her bed—spending every day and every night crying. Her father could not deal with it and departed to a local bar to escape nightly. That left Jessica all by herself with no one to talk to. Her loneliness and feelings of being unloved amplified.

The next few months were a little better. Her mother started taking some medication to calm her nerves and could now get out of bed and lounge around the house. However, she moved slowly, and she had very little expression on her face, almost zombie-like. Her mother's doctor recommended grief counseling for the family, but her parents refused.

Her father started working from home. Although her parents were both physically there, they were emotionally checked out. The conversations they did have centered around her father's work and her mother's pills. Occasionally, they would bring up Jonathon, saying what a perfect son he was and how the house is dead now that he's gone.

Jessica remembered wanting to yell, "I'm here. I'm alive. Pay attention to me!"

Jessica became more and more withdrawn as the feelings of being unloved grew stronger in her mind. She wondered what was wrong with her. She didn't know why she was so unlovable.

Six months after Jonathon's death, her mother came back to life. She began to cook and clean again. Occasionally, she would even ask Jessica to come and watch TV with her. Her father even looked happier somehow.

Jessica was confused but didn't care. She was just happy to have some attention from her parents again.

Later that month, her parents sat her down to announce the great news. Her mom exclaimed, "Our family has been saved! We will have life in this house again!" Jessica's mom was pregnant, and they were expecting a baby in January.

Jessica was in shock. She didn't know what to say. She didn't know what to feel. "A baby? Life in this house again? I'm alive! I have always been alive! Doesn't my life count?" Jessica remembered thinking.

Fast-forward a few years later; Jessica reports feeling even more distant from her parents. They spent so much time and attention on Jennifer that they rarely noticed Jessica's presence. Sure, they pretended to include her in on their activities sometimes, but the offers were so fake that they angered Jessica even more.

Session Five Notes

Jessica reports feeling even more neglected within the last six months. Jennifer is now in first grade and her parents are spending even more time with her. This leaves little time for Jessica. Her anger and resentment have been growing stronger, and it's affecting her attitude at school and at home. Jessica feels like she has this monster inside her that just wants to come out and unleash its anger onto the world. Recently, Jessica has been unable to control herself and has gotten into several fights.

Private Session with Jessica's Parents

Both parents agreed and confirmed Jessica's story that they were emotionally unavailable the months after Jonathon's death. They felt bad about it and tried to make it up to Jessica. However, most of the time, their efforts were shot down or ignored. Jessica would often tell them, "I'm doing fine. I like being by myself." They thought the best they could do for her was to allow her to be herself as she dealt with her grief in her own way.

This pattern persisted for years to come. Jessica was always by herself, doing her own thing. Her mother said, "She was such a good student and never complained about anything. We thought she was just an introvert... a loner. Every time we asked her to do something with us, she would say 'no.' We didn't want to force anything on her."

Jessica agreed with this story but added that she felt the invitations were never sincere. Jessica insisted that if they loved her, they would understand her better.

Session Six to Twelve Notes

The next few sessions were spent working with Jessica and her parents individually to help them process the pain of Jonathon's death and the rift in their relationships. Jessica could finally let go of her anger toward her parents and work through her grief of losing her brother. She also let go of the resentment toward Jennifer.

Three-Month Follow-Up

Jessica and her parents' relationship is improving steadily. Jessica can now see that they do love her and value her as a family member. Jessica also saw how her actions played a role in her feeling unloved. Her lack of willingness to take part in family activities and her constantly telling them she enjoyed being by herself caused a lot of misunderstanding and pain. Jessica learned that she needed to be an active participant in creating the life she wanted. Jessica also reports that she's getting along better with Jennifer.

Six-Month Follow-Up

Jessica joined the art club at school and now has several close friends. She reports being much happier with life. The anger is no longer present. Jessica feels at peace. Her relationship with her parents and Jennifer is still improving. In fact, Jessica is now teaching Jennifer how to draw.

Lesson Learned

This is a strong lesson in how you create your own reality. Because of Jonathon's death and the subsequent months afterward, Jessica learned to believe that she was not loved. Lost in their pain, Jessica's parents left her alone, causing her to feel alone, lonely and unlovable.

Once Jessica believed that she was unloved, her subconscious mind went into high gear, looking for evidence to support her beliefs. Every time her parents weren't paying attention to her was another piece of evidence to validate her beliefs. When her parents attempted to connect with her, Jessica refused.

Jessica's belief that she was not loved, and that she was unlovable made it impossible for her to see that these were loving actions directed toward her. Rather, she thought they were fake attempts, and she became lonelier and angrier.

Jessica's experience is a great example of why professional help is important after trauma. The family could have grieved together and possibly become closer, rather than falling apart. Further, Jessica might also have an easier time accepting Jennifer from the start if Jessica felt safe and secure in her relationship with her parents.

You are in charge of creating your reality. Whatever you focus on becomes your experience. If you focus on the negative aspects of an event, your experience will be negative. The more you focus on the negative aspects, the stronger your negative beliefs will become.

> **REMEMBER**: *Whether you spend your time and energy focusing on the negatives or the positives of any situation, you will spend your time and energy in some way. Why not focus on the positive aspects rather than the negatives and create happy experiences for yourself?*

You deserve to be happy, and you are in charge of your happiness.

Self-Reflection

1. What is your biggest take-away from this chapter?
2. How can you use what you've just learned to take charge of your mind and be a happier, more confident you?

CHAPTER EIGHT

I'm Not Safe

I'm not safe can refer to both physical safety and emotional safety and often shows up as:

- People want to hurt me physically or emotionally.
- I'm too weak to defend myself.
- People are evil.
- People take advantage of me.
- The world is so scary.
- It's me against the world.
- I can't trust anyone.

Case Study: Helpless Hailey
Client: Hailey   Age: 13

Presenting Problem

Hailey was brought in by her mother, Pamela, because she has become increasingly fearful of being alone. Hailey normally sleeps with her door closed and her lights off. One day, for no apparent reason, Hailey had a very rough, sleepless night. From that night on, she had to keep the door open and the lights on when she went to bed. Over the next few months, she became more anxious and afraid.

Hailey's anxiety and fear of being alone are so high that she cannot be by herself for more than 10-15 minutes without going into an anxious state that requires her mother's intervention. She constantly follows her mother and her fifteen-year-old brother, Jack, around the house. Recently, Hailey started begging to sleep in her mom's room. Her brother is resentful because he lost a significant amount of freedom as he now has to "babysit" her.

Family History

Hailey is the youngest of two siblings being raised by a single mom. Hailey's father passed away from cancer when she was an infant. Both Hailey and her brother were too young to understand the impact at the time of their father's death. Pamela has never remarried and is a devoted mother.

Social History

Hailey is a "B" student with many close friends at school and church. She gets along well with her peers and adults. She has been attending the same church weekly for many years and until four months ago, was highly active in her church's youth group. Now, Hailey prefers to be home with her family.

Words Hailey Often Heard Others Used to Describe Her

Nice, helpful, friendly, funny, outgoing, cheerful

Words Hailey Uses to Describe Herself

Average, anxious, scared all the time, afraid to be alone, childish, something is wrong with me

Session One Notes

Hailey is a sweet girl with a ready smile and a soft voice. She was a little nervous at first but warmed up easily. She stated, "I'm will do what you tell me because I'm tired of being scared."

Hailey denied any abuse, trauma, or significant events in her life. She reported no use of alcohol or drugs.

Hailey is confused and frustrated because she can't understand why this is happening. She feels tired of being scared and wants to go back to her normal life. Life was good for Hailey until four months ago when she could not sleep one night. As Hailey tossed and turned in her bed, she saw what she thought were shadows moving along her walls. She didn't think much of it at first because she knew she was tired. She figured her eyes were playing tricks on her.

As the night progressed, Hailey would go in and out of sleep. Each time she woke up, she would become more and more anxious, and the shadow movements became more and more pronounced.

At one point, Hailey was certain there was someone in her room. She grabbed her cell phone and used the flashlight function to check her room and made sure no one was there.

The next night, Hailey had difficulty falling asleep again. However, this time, Hailey felt anxious immediately and had to open her door and turn her lights on for comfort. This started Hailey's new pattern of sleeping with her door open and her lights on.

A few weeks later, Hailey was studying in her room as she has always done before. Her mother was making dinner downstairs and her brother was in the living room, watching TV. Again, for no apparent reason, Hailey felt significant anxiety and fear that something was wrong. She ran downstairs to check on her mother and brother. For the rest of the night, Hailey stayed close to her mother.

Hailey started spending less and less time alone. At first, Pamela liked the company and was enjoying this increased mother daughter bonding experience. She didn't realize there was a problem until Jack brought it up at dinner one night. Jack told Pamela he was sick and tired of Hailey always following him around. He felt he didn't have any freedom because everywhere he was, Hailey was right there by his side. He felt suffocated. He demanded that it stop.

For the first time, Pamela realized that this bonding experience was, in fact, Hailey being very clingy. Looking back, Pamela realized that Hailey never spent time alone anymore, except for bedtime. Pamela also never thought much about Hailey's new sleeping preference, but in retrospect, everything became clearer.

To help Hailey, Pamela started becoming firmer, insisting Hailey practice spending some time alone each day. Each time Hailey tried to spend time alone, it only lasted about fifteen minutes. She would then run to Pamela, crying and hyperventilating. Pamela had to help guide her with deep breathing exercises to calm her down.

When Hailey started begging to sleep with her mother, Pamela finally realized the severity of the problem and sought help.

Although there were no real significant events that caused Hailey to experience that first sleepless night, that night was so traumatic for her. In those in-between sleep states, Hailey felt very anxious and unsafe.

Because this event was so significant and so specific, we were able to use a simple method to scramble this movie in her mind. At the end of the session, Hailey left feeling more confident in herself.

The next morning, Pamela called to tell me that Hailey slept with only a night light on. She went to bed feeling a little nervous, but very excited to see if the session helped. This was Hailey's first night of rested sleep in a long time.

Session Two Notes

The following week, Hailey came back with a lot of eagerness to continue our work together. She reported that she has been able to sleep with the lights off for the last three nights. However, she was still afraid to be by herself and still spent much of her time following her mom and brother around. We spent the rest of the session working on changing her mindset to accept that she is courageous and safe.

Root Cause

During session three, we discovered an incident that happened when Hailey was three years old. Hailey went to play in the backyard by herself. She has done this many times before.

However, when she came back into the house this time, she could not find her mother or brother. She called out for them and searched the whole house. She was terrified because she couldn't find them. In that instance, Hailey was certain that someone had come in and kidnapped them. She was afraid she would never see them again.

Hailey recalled feeling extremely alone and terrified that the people who kidnapped her mother and brother would come back for her. She remembered being too scared to cry or move. Every single noise she heard, she believed to be the kidnapper coming back for her.

The next thing she remembered, Hailey woke up in the dark, in her own bed, with a lot of pain to her forehead. She screamed out for her mom and her mom came running to her.

Hailey later found out that her mother and brother had just stepped outside of their house to say "hi" to the new neighbors. Hailey's mom saw she was enjoying playing in the backyard and didn't want to interrupt her.

When her mom came back inside the house, she found Hailey sleeping by the stairs and brought her to her bed. Evidently, she must have passed out in fear and hit her head, but her mom was unaware. She just thought Hailey fell asleep while waiting for them to come in and took her to bed.

Because the event was so significant and so specific, we were able to scramble it easily. Hailey was able to see the full picture and accepted that she was safe, and her mother and brother were also safe the whole time.

Once Hailey fully understood and accepted the reality of the situation, she was able to move on.

Three-Month Follow-Up

Life has returned to normal for Hailey and her family. Hailey reported being able to sleep with the lights off and be comfortable by herself. When the old fear tried to come back, she would close her eyes and imagine that she was watching an unpleasant movie and turn it off.

Occasionally, she would imagine herself turning off the old movie and switching to her favorite TV show. That brought her peace and calmness immediately. Using this simple technique has helped Hailey to take control of her life. She is now actively engaging in her youth group even more.

Hailey's mom reported an interesting side note: Haley's motivation and focus have increased significantly. She is now getting four "A's" and two "B's" in her classes at school.

Lesson Learned

This is a powerful lesson in what our minds can do to hold us hostage. While Hailey experienced no "real" trauma, her imagination and misguided beliefs when she was a toddler created a deep-rooted belief that she was not safe.

Once that belief was created and placed in her IC, it ran in the background, collecting evidence to support it. I'm certain there were many smaller incidences that validated that belief for Hailey, but the night when she couldn't sleep definitely brought this old, hidden belief to the forefront of Hailey's subconscious mind. The Stranger Danger Protocol was on high alert and Hailey experienced significant fear throughout her day. She had to stay by her mom's side for safety.

Once the emotions attached to this belief were neutralized, Hailey was able to realize and accept that she and her loved ones were safe. The Stranger Danger Protocol was turned off and Hailey was once again at peace.

REMEMBER: *Your subconscious mind does not know how to differentiate between what's real and what's vividly imagined. To your subconscious mind, it's the same.*

In Hailey's case, her vivid imagination at age three caused her significant pain and grief later on in her life.

Be kind to yourself. If you catch yourself creating scary what-if scenarios in your head or replaying painful experiences of your past, tell yourself to stop. Give yourself permission to focus on something different. Whatever you focus on becomes bigger. Why not focus on the things that bring you happiness?

I hope this book and the four case studies in this book helped you to understand how powerful your mind is and how you can play a significant role in creating your life experiences.

REMEMBER: *You are the boss of your mind. It is up to you to give your assistant the commands that bring you closer and closer to your goals and dreams.*

If you find yourself drifting away from your goals or dreams, pause, re-evaluate, and re-decide on a course of action that best serves your needs. You can learn to take control of your feelings, thoughts, and actions. You can learn to take control of your life.

Self-Reflection

1. What is your biggest take-away from this chapter?
2. How can you use what you've just learned to take charge of your mind and be a happier, more confident you

Jump-Start Your Confidence & Boost Your Self-Esteem

A Guide for Teen Girls: Unleash Your Inner Superpowers to Destroy Fear and Self-Doubt, and Build Unshakable Confidence

Book 3 to 3

Jacqui Letran

DUNEDIN, FLORIDA

Table of Contents

Book Three: Jump-Start Your Confidence

Introduction

D o you often feel as though other people are better than you? Does it seem they are more carefree, more outgoing, and more confident? They make friends easily and good things seem to happen for them all the time. They are fun, witty, and full of charm. Everywhere they go, people are drawn to them. They do what they want and say what they think.

These positive, likable traits seem to come so naturally for them. But for you, life is filled with anxiety, fear, and self-doubt. What is their secret? How can they talk to anyone about anything with ease, while it's a significant struggle for you to just be in the presence of others, let alone carry on a conversation?

You dream of being different. You dream of being comfortable in your own skin. You dream of creating meaningful relationships, going after what you want with confidence, and feeling happy and satisfied with your everyday life. But your fear and self-doubt are holding you back, causing you to feel trapped and powerless to change your situation. You're left feeling sad, lonely, and insecure about yourself and your life.

What if there was a way to change all of that? What if you could destroy your fear and self-doubt and be strong and self-assured instead? What would it be like if you could go into any situation with excitement, courage, and confidence?

Imagine what your life would look like and what you could achieve.

Just imagine.

I will let you in on a little secret. That excitement, courage, and confidence which you admire in others are skills that you can learn.

Sure, there are some people for whom these traits come naturally, but if you were not born with these traits, you can learn them. The thing is, you can learn to destroy your fear and self-doubt and go after whatever you want with confidence. You can learn to be comfortable in your own skin and be completely at ease while expressing yourself.

You were born with all the resources—or Inner Superpowers (ISPs)—you need to be happy, resilient, and successful in life. The problem is that you have not been aware of these ISPs, nor how to use them.

Maybe you saw a glimpse of them here and there, but you didn't recognize their power or have faith in them. If you don't know what your ISPs are, how can you tap into them consistently and achieve the results you want and deserve?

In this book, you will learn:

- The seven Inner Superpowers guaranteed to destroy your fear and self-doubt.
- Create a strong sense of self-esteem and unshakable confidence.
- How to connect to and strengthen your Inner Superpowers.
- How to tap into and unleash your Inner Superpowers whenever you want to.
- How to live within your full power and be happy, confident, and successful in life—and so much more!

You have so many Inner Superpowers that make you wonderful in every way. In this book, I have chosen to share seven specific ISPs because these seven are your best bet for destroying fear and self-doubt.

There is much written about each of these ISPs and each ISPs can be a stand-alone book. However, I know your time is valuable and you have other responsibilities and activities to tend to. Therefore, you'll find that these chapters are brief and to the point.

I will present enough information for you to understand your ISPs without bogging you down with too much information. By reading this book and completing the activities within each section, you will learn how to tap into these ISPs consistently, harness them, and unleash them whenever you want. You can learn how to go after what you want with confidence and create that happy and successful life you've been dreaming about.

NOTE: To get the most benefit from this book, work on each Inner Superpower in the order presented, as the concepts of each build to the next.

CHAPTER ONE

It's All in Your Mind

Your mind has everything to do with your Inner Superpowers. It is essential for you to understand how your mind works so you can truly tap into it.

In this book, I will give you an overview of the inner workings of your mind. If you would like to go deeper into this topic, you can reread the second book in this series, entitled I would, but my DAMN MIND won't let me, where this topic is discussed in more depth.

Your Conscious and Subconscious Mind

Your conscious mind is your logical mind. It's the part of your mind that you are aware of. It's the part of your mind that you use when you focus on things or learn new things.

For example, your conscious mind helps you to learn how to play a sport, such as tennis. When you are in the learning phase, you consciously focus on learning proper techniques, such as how to hold the racquet properly, how to position your body to prepare for the incoming ball, and the proper way to move your body to create an effective swing. These thoughts and actions are the work of your conscious mind—something you are aware of and actively focusing on.

Your conscious mind is also responsible for helping you make decisions based on the things in front of you and the things you've learned from previous experiences. It is the part of your mind that makes simple decisions such as, "I want to wear shorts today because it's a warm day."

It also makes more complex decisions such as, "Should I lie to my mom so I can get out of trouble, but risk having her find out and getting even more upset with me?"

Your conscious mind does not work fully until around seven years old. This is why you believed in the Tooth Fairy, the Easter Bunny, and Santa Claus (not to mention your imaginary best friend) when you were a little kid. Before seven, you don't have a fully working logical mind that says, "That's not true because I've learned so-and-so and that doesn't match what I've learned."

As you get older and your conscious mind develops more and more, you begin to question whether those beliefs are true. Eventually, you stop believing in the Tooth Fairy, the Easter Bunny, and Santa Claus because your conscious mind is fully formed, and you can logically decide based on the facts you have learned over the years.

Your subconscious mind differs greatly from your conscious mind. The first important difference is that you are not aware of, nor can you control, what happens in your subconscious mind. Everything that happens in the subconscious part of your mind is happening without you knowing and without your control. In fact, everything that happens in your subconscious mind happens automatically, as if it's a program running on autopilot in the background.

Your subconscious mind works immediately at birth and one of its biggest jobs is to keep you alive and safe. However, to the subconscious mind, "safe" doesn't mean "safe" the way you probably define it today. Instead, "safe" means "Do not change. Stay exactly the way you are. Change is scary. Change is dangerous. If you try to change, you will get hurt."

When you are doing something new or outside of your belief system, your subconscious mind freaks out. It believes that you are putting yourself at risk for failure, rejection, or pain. So, it will do whatever it can to get you back to your "safe" place, which means going back to your old ways and staying exactly how you are right now.

To get you back to your "safe" place, your subconscious mind uses fear tactics to prevent you from taking actions and moving forward. It will do whatever it needs to do to get you to stop doing that new activity and return you to where you were. This is why a lot of people report feeling "stuck" when they are dealing with unhappy or difficult situations.

How many times have you wanted to do something, especially something new and a little scary, and immediately started feeling anxious and full of self-doubt? Even though you really wanted to do that thing, all you could think of is how you could end up failing, hurting, or embarrassing yourself. Instead of following through and doing what you wanted to do, you stop and retreat to your familiar pattern.

That's your subconscious mind at work. Your subconscious mind knows when you are fearful or anxious, chances are you'll stop what you're thinking about doing or attempting to do and go back to your old ways, the "safe" and familiar ways. Every time you attempt something and retreat, you reinforce your beliefs of "I can't" or "This is who I am."

Your Subconscious Mind Simplified

Let's explore your subconscious mind a little more; once you understand how your subconscious mind works, it will be so much easier to access your Inner Superpowers.

First, I want you to think of your subconscious mind as a collection of movies within a movie library. In this movie library, there are hundreds of thousands of movies—all starring YOU! Imagine there's a DVD for everything you have ever thought, felt, or done. That's a lot of DVDs, isn't it?

In your movie library is your personal assistant, which is really your subconscious mind. Its job is to continue to record your movies, store them, and replay them at the right time for you. In addition, your subconscious mind has a bigger job: to keep you safe. Unfortunately, more often than not, that means creating anxiety, fear, and self-doubt to prevent you from moving into the perceived unsafe territory.

Also, your subconscious mind is programmed to give you whatever experience you're looking for in the easiest, quickest way possible. Yes, you read that right! Your subconscious mind is programmed to give you whatever experience you're looking for, in the easiest, quickest way possible—as long as the thing you want matches your belief system. How you have perceived all of your experiences so far has been because of the requests you have made to your subconscious mind.

You might think, "But I didn't ask for all the stress or pain that I'm experiencing, nor for all those judgments I've been receiving."

While it might not seem like you've asked for those experiences, you did. You didn't know that you were asking for them because you don't fully understand how your mind works, or the enormous potential of your Inner Superpowers yet. (Hint: They are the key to radically changing how you ask for future experiences!).

Let me explain how you've been asking your mind for your experiences so far. Every single thought and feeling you have is a direct command to your subconscious mind, "This is the experience I want to have. Give me this experience."

Therefore, when you were getting ready for that presentation in class and you imagined how nervous you will be when it's your turn, you gave your subconscious mind these commands, "I want to be nervous during the presentation. This is the experience that I want. Give me this experience. Make sure I'm nervous during the presentation."

Being a loyal and faithful assistant, your subconscious mind goes to work immediately and scans your environment, searching for anything that could cause you to be nervous. The moment it finds something that could cause you to feel nervous, it directs all your attention to that thing.

At the same time, your subconscious mind will look into your movie library, looking for past movies that could cause you to feel nervous about your current situation. It will replay those movies for you automatically in the background of your mind. In addition, it creates a new movie of what could happen in your future based on your past experiences and the current experience you're asking for.

Not only does your subconscious replay all the times you were nervous presenting in front of the class, but it also starts playing the new movie it just made of you stumbling on your words and failing miserably during your presentation today. By the time it's your turn to present, you have become so nervous that all you can focus on is the sweatiness of your palms, the shakiness of your voice, and all those judgmental looks from your classmates.

The good news is that once you understand your subconscious mind and your Inner Superpowers, you can purposefully send the right commands to your subconscious mind in a positive and powerful way. That way, your subconscious mind can bring you a much better experience than what you have been through in the past.

A moment ago, I mentioned that your subconscious mind's job is to give you the experience you're looking for as long as it matches your current belief system. Your belief system is the program of your subconscious mind that runs on autopilot in the background. Whatever you believe is true is what your subconscious mind will continuously look for evidence of.

Similar to the concept that all thoughts and feelings are direct commands to your subconscious mind ("This is the experience I want; give me this experience."), your belief systems are also direct commands. However, belief systems are more powerful because they run automatically in the back of your mind all day. You don't even have to request these experiences actively through your thoughts and feelings.

As humans, we have this need to be right and our subconscious mind will work hard to make sure that this need is fulfilled. To complete this task, your subconscious mind will generalize, distort, or delete details so that the only experiences you have will match your belief system.

For example, if you have a belief that you are forgetful, your subconscious mind will ignore each instance of you remembering details or will distort it and call it "pure luck" or "a coincidence" when you catch yourself remembering something. You remember so much more than you forget, but when you forget something, your subconscious mind will happily bring it to your awareness.

Another example of how your subconscious mind will make sure your experiences match your beliefs is through generalization. Let's say a dog bite you when you were young, and that experience caused you significant pain and fear. To protect you from another similar painful episode, your mind might create the generalization that "all dogs are mean and will bite you." This causes you to hate dogs and you feel fearful whenever you're around any dog.

Unfortunately, dogs are great at picking up on when someone doesn't like them or when someone is fearful of them. To protect themselves, dogs will act aggressively when you are nearby because they sense your dislike and fear. This generalization allows you to be right and even influences the world around you (a dog in this case) to provide you with the experience that "all dogs are mean," when in fact, most dogs are rather sweet.

Commanding Your Subconscious Mind

A moment ago, you learned that every thought you have and every feeling you feel is a command to your subconscious mind to give you more of the same experience.

Here are three more important details for you to command your mind effectively:

Negative Commands Confuse Your Mind

Your subconscious mind does not know how to process negative commands. Negative commands are commands such as, "I don't want" or "I'm no longer" or "I'm not." Basically, they are any command that focuses on what you are *not*, or what you *don't* want. This is because for your subconscious mind to fully understand your command, it has to create a picture or to clearly "see" the experience you're looking for.

Let's say you wanted your brother to bring you your blue sweater, and you said to him, "Can you go to my room and bring me my sweater? I don't want the orange one." What are the chances that your brother would know you want him to bring you the *blue* sweater? Pretty slim—unless you only have two sweaters, an orange one and a blue one. Even then, wouldn't it be better to say to him, "Bring me the blue sweater," so he knows what color to look for and can find it quickly for you?

Your subconscious mind works the same way. When you give the command, "I don't want to be sad," it might seem like a good command at first because you don't want to be sad. But that command doesn't help your mind understand your true request. All it knows is that you don't want the experience of being sad, but it does not understand what experience you want instead. Your subconscious mind doesn't know if you want to feel angry, overwhelmed, unmotivated, disgusted, or many other feelings.

To help your subconscious mind understand your command, it creates a picture for each of the words in the command that can have an associated image, which are "I" and "sad" in this example. The mental picture of this command is, therefore, an image of you being sad. Then, the command becomes, "I want to be sad."

It is so important to focus on what you want rather than what you don't want. If you gave the command, "I want to be happy," or "I want to be relaxed," your subconscious mind would understand it and could bring that to you easily.

Weak Versus Strong Commands

Your commands could be viewed as strong or weak commands. Strong commands get your subconscious mind's attention immediately and direct your subconscious mind effectively.

One way to think about this is by knowing that you are the boss of your mind. As a boss, you can be firm or weak with your commands. To command your subconscious mind effectively and get your desired results, choose strong, powerful commands. Commands such as, "I choose," "I'm ready," "I'm determined," or "I'm committed to," are very strong commands.

Think about it. When you say, "I am determined to be an A student," how does that look in your mind's eye? How does that feel?

Now, try for the same outcome, but with a weaker command. "I hope I'll be an A student." How is this picture different in your mind? How does this command make you feel?

In the "determined" picture, you are in charge of your outcome. Chances are you'll see yourself confidently going after what you want to achieve. You might see yourself putting energy and effort into studying. You might see yourself pushing through barriers to achieve success.

In the "hope" picture, you might see yourself as uncertain as you attempt to work toward your goal. The energy and effort you're putting into those activities are not as strong or as persistent as your "determined" picture. Sure, you may do some work, but you'll leave more to chance.

Weak commands to avoid are commands such as "I wish," "I want," or "I hope." When you wish, want, or hope for a result, your attitude about how to proceed isn't as solid or as powerful as when you are ready, determined, or committed to your goal.

Vague Comparative Commands Don't Help

Your subconscious mind is very literal, which could cause it to believe that it has successfully given you the experiences you've asked for when, in fact, it hasn't When you give your subconscious mind a Vague Comparative Command that sounds like, "I wish I had more money," the "more money" part of that sentence is a comparison of one thing to another. Yet, it doesn't really identify what it's being compared to.

What does "more money" mean, exactly? More money than you've had in your life? More money than whom? If you had one penny more than you did a minute ago, you do, in fact, have more money, but I doubt that's what your intention was when you made the request.

If you said, "I am determined to have $100 more than I have right now," your subconscious mind knows exactly what you want, doesn't it?

Suppose you give your subconscious mind the command, "I want to be happier." Again, happier than when? Happier than whom? To your subconscious mind, if you are happier now than you were last week (when you were overwhelmingly depressed), then it would believe that it has already successfully delivered the experience you're asking for and it doesn't have to do anything else other than to continue to give you the same experience.

Strong, powerful, and clear commands such as, "I am committed to being happy," or "I'm ready to be happy," are great alternatives. When you use these commands, your subconscious mind will get busy looking for reasons for you to be happy in that moment and evidence that you are committed to your happiness.

Remember, to give your subconscious mind the most powerful commands:

1. Focus on your desired outcome and be specific.
2. Stop focusing on the things you don't want or the condition you want to move away from.
3. Use strong command words such as "choose," "ready to," "committed to," and "determined to."
4. Avoid Vague Comparative Commands such as "more" or "better than." If you give a comparative command, it is best to give a specific comparison.

Stop Watching Those Crappy Movies

Think of a type of movie that you absolutely hate to watch because it's uncomfortable, or it stresses you out. For me, it's gory, violent movies. For the sake of this example, let's pretend that you also hate to watch gory, violent movies.

Now, imagine you just had a very stressful day, and you want to relax and watch something on TV to take your mind off your stress. You sit down on your couch and turn on the television. In front of you is the goriest, most violent movie you have ever seen and the sound of people screaming in pain is blasting loudly. What would you do in that instance?

Chances are you would turn the TV off, change the channel, or go do something else. Would you ever sit in front of that television screen and think, "Please let this movie end. I can't stand this movie. I feel so helpless that this movie is playing in front of me. There is nothing I can do to stop this movie. I'm just a victim."

Of course, you wouldn't think these thoughts in this situation! That would be silly because you have the power to leave, turn the TV off, or change the channel. At that moment, you would take control and be the boss of that situation, wouldn't you?

What if I told you that you do, in fact, sit in front of unpleasant movies and act like a powerless victim quite often? Would it surprise you to know that you do this? Well, my dear reader, you do, in fact, do this a lot.

How often do you replay a scene of a real or perceived failure in your mind? What about recalling every single detail of an argument, or how someone once mistreated you? How many times have you replayed the movie where you embarrassed yourself in front of your friends or classmates? When you think about those events, how did you feel? Did you feel powerful and confident, or did you find yourself full of anxiety, fear, or self-doubt?

Remember earlier, when I said your subconscious mind is a room full of movies about you? Every time you replay an argument or beat yourself up for something that happened in the past, all you are doing is replaying that crappy movie, repeatedly, and watching it as if you are powerless to change the channel. You play some movies so many times they have found their way onto your automatic "favorite playlist."

You don't have to watch those movies or listen to the recording of them anymore. You can turn them off. Just like a television, you have different channels in your mind. If you have an experience you don't like, be willing to change the station to something else or turn the television off completely. I will show you how to do this when I teach you about your Inner Superpowers.

I hope by now, you are getting a lot of "Ah-Ha!" moments and things are making sense for you. Let's dive into those Inner Superpowers now, so you can start taking charge of yourself and your life.

Self-Reflection

Take five minutes to think about how your life will look once you understand your Inner Superpowers and can tap into them consistently to destroy your fear and self-doubt. What would that look like? What would you do next? How would your life be different?

Use your imagination and have fun with this self-reflection. Write down all the wonderful things you can do now because you are strong, confident, and courageous. Remember to dream big!

CHAPTER TWO

The Power of Words

Words are one of our greatest and most frequently used Inner Superpowers. Words can create significant insecurities, destroy relationships, and tear families apart. Words can also have an equally positive effect. It can give a hopeless person hope, heal a broken heart, and give someone the power and courage to pursue their dreams.

You might be thinking, "Wait a minute—aren't words external? How can they be an Inner Superpower?"

Great questions! Words are an Inner Superpower because your words come from within yourself. These include the words you speak out loud, but more importantly, also the words you say to yourself when you think and analyze situations.

Why Words Are a Superpower

Have you ever done something that you were really proud of and were really excited to share that achievement with your friends and family? However, the moment you shared your accomplishment with someone, you immediately feel deflated, embarrassed, or maybe even sad.

Perhaps the words they responded with made you feel criticized. Perhaps the words they used made you feel as though you're not good enough. You might start to doubt yourself or even call yourself names. You might wonder if you are lame or even stupid for being so proud of something that no one else seemed to care about.

You are not alone in this pattern of thinking and feeling. We all have had similar negative thoughts in the back of our minds at different times that caused us to feel sad, scared, uncomfortable, or full of self-doubt. How destructive is that way of thinking?

Just a moment ago, you were feeling great. But because someone said harsh or unsupportive words to you, your happiness level plummeted. Not only did your happiness level plummet, but perhaps your self-belief and self-confidence took a dive just as quickly. Often, you will start using negative words to yourself after these types of events. Maybe you think, "I'm a loser. No one cares about me or what I do."

Those silent conversations you have with yourself are exceptionally powerful because you may not even realize that they are happening. Even so, your subconscious mind is paying attention and is looking for evidence to fulfill your request to experience being a loser that no one cares about.

All of this works together to create significant negative emotions that result in you doubting yourself, your abilities, and maybe even your self-worth. That's the power of words. They can take you from total excitement and happiness to sadness, fear, and self-doubt in a flash.

The good news is that words can also have a powerfully positive effect. Imagine a time that you felt down, frustrated, isolated, and alone. Now, imagine that someone reached out to you and said just the right words—words you desperately wanted or needed to hear at that moment.

Perhaps you were feeling a lot of pain and uncertainty and a friend reached out to you and said, "You're going to be OK. I'm here for you." You went from feeling sad, alone, or frustrated to feeling a lot better almost immediately. Perhaps you might even feel safe, supported, loved, or happy. Because of these kind and supportive words, your mood changed; and it changed at the speed of thought!

You start seeing possibilities where there were only limitations before. Rather than retreating, you look for ways to move past this block. You feel motivated. You see solutions easily and you feel confident in your ability to solve your problems, or maybe you see a way out. This is the positive power of words!

Word Filters

Your words have immense powers. Whatever words you use to express your thoughts or feelings, whether out loud or silently to yourself, are the same words that create your reality and life experiences. In this way, it is very similar to editing a picture using a filter app.

Imagine taking a vibrant and colorful photo and putting a black and white filter on it. What would happen? Would your picture remain vibrant and colorful, or would it change into a black-and-white picture? If you are editing a photo using a particular filter and you don't like the result, are you going to say, "Oh, well. There's nothing I could do about it"? Or would you try out a different filter? Most likely, you would try a different filter or at least revert to the original picture.

Our life experiences are very similar to that. Just imagine your words are the filters, or "Word Filters," and your life experiences are the photos. Whatever Word Filters you choose to put on your life experiences will become the result you see in your "photos," which is your reality. When you have an experience you don't like, be willing to play around with different Word Filters and create the pictures you want at that moment.

For example, let's say you tried out for a lead role in your school play, and you were not chosen. The Word Filters that naturally pop up for you might sound like, "I don't deserve that part because I'm a terrible actor. Everyone else is so much better than me. Who am I kidding? I'm no good at this. Why do I even bother?" When you use these Word Filters to view your experience, how do you feel? Do you feel positive and encouraged, or do you feel sad and deflated?

Instead of allowing your old Word Filters to control your mood, what if you decided to use your Inner Superpower of Words to express yourself? What if you choose to think or say, "That actor got the role because they have three more years of experience than I do. I am a beginner, and I am committed to learning and practicing so I can be my best," or "I am not the right person for this part and the right part for me will come along." When you use these Word Filters, how do you feel? Do you feel sad and deflated, or do you feel motivated to improve yourself and inspired to look for new opportunities?

The reality of the situation is that you did not get the lead role. However, how you choose to view that event will either lift you up and prepare you for the next opportunity or drag you down and discourage your ambitions. The choice is yours.

Your words are that powerful. And if you are careless with your words, you can create unwanted (and unnecessary!) pain and misery for yourself and others around you. Be purposeful in the words you use to create the experiences you want for yourself and those you care about. Choose words that are supportive, encouraging, and inspiring when you speak to yourself and others. You can create your experiences by selecting the words that empower you.

The Power of "I AM"

In the English language, the two most powerful words, when used together, are the words "I AM." Whatever you put behind "I AM" becomes your reality. The words that immediately follow "I AM" are your declaration to your subconscious mind and the Universe: "This is who I am. Make sure I have this experience."

Let's say you're going to a party and you're feeling a little nervous. You worry that you'll have a bad time because you believe people don't like you or that you are awkward and won't fit in. Imagine entering the party with these thoughts, "I AM going to be so uncomfortable. I AM so nervous. I AM going to feel and act so awkward."

These are your declarations and commands to your subconscious mind to make sure you have these experiences. Your subconscious mind will hear those thoughts as commands, "I want to have a bad time. Make sure I feel like I don't fit in. Make sure I feel so uncomfortable, nervous, and awkward."

Being that dedicated assistant, your subconscious mind will go to work and adjust your environment so that no matter where you look, you will get to experience the party through the Word Filters of your negative "I AM" commands.

As you sit in the corner by yourself, looking nervously around, you happen to lock eyes with someone who has an unpleasant expression on her face; maybe you see it as a disgusted expression. Immediately, you start thinking, "I KNEW IT! I shouldn't be here. Everyone thinks I'm a weirdo. What was I thinking? I'm so stupid to think I could fit in or have fun." Look what has happened—a new flood of negative commands that will reinforce your experience and your beliefs!

How damaging are your words to your confidence and self-esteem? Because you glanced up and saw someone with an unpleasant expression on her face and the Word Filters you're using are negative ones, you instantly came to a destructive conclusion that caused you to feel worse about yourself and your situation.

In reality, perhaps that girl was thinking, "I got all dressed up for Tommy and he won't even look at me. He doesn't think I'm attractive." Or maybe she's thinking, "OMG, I forgot to turn the curling iron off at home. I'm going to burn the house down! I always do stupid things like this," and the disgusted look on her face reflects her fear and her own self-judgments, which has nothing to do with you at all.

These two examples show how we are all "in our own minds," thinking about our problems. The experiences we have are of our own creation based on the words we choose when we talk to ourselves. We are all guilty of creating these negative stories in our minds. We make ourselves fearful, sad, or anxious for no reason other than because we don't feel good about ourselves in those moments and we are not fully aware of the power of our words.

How to Destroy Fear and Self-Doubt Using the Power of Words

If you feel nervous at any event or situation, you can take control by unleashing your Inner Superpower of Words and select a different set of Word Filters. Maybe you can choose a couple of these different Word Filters instead:

- "I AM OK. Everything will be OK."
- "I AM willing to have fun."
- "I AM calm."
- "I AM excited to try something new."
- "I AM courageous."
- "I AM excited to meet new people."
- "I AM ready to enjoy myself."

When you choose positive Word Filters like these, you give your subconscious mind an entirely different set of commands. You are telling your subconscious mind to use the lenses that allow you to have positive experiences. You might even find yourself having fun and connecting with people like never before because you have actively chosen to use your Inner Superpower of Words to create meaningful experiences for yourself.

Now that you are aware of the Inner Superpower of Words, I encourage you to go through the following exercises to help you master this power. With practice, you can easily and effectively destroy your fear and self-doubt.

Self-Reflection

Spend a few minutes answering these questions and coming up with examples for the following:

1. On a scale of 0 to 10 (with 10 being the highest), how aware were you of how your words impacted yourself and others prior to reading this chapter? How aware are you now?

2. List two examples of how the words you've been using created pain for yourself.

3. List two examples of how the words you've been using created pain for someone else.

4. List two examples of how the words you've been using have supported, inspired, or motivated yourself.

5. List two examples of how the words you've been using have supported, inspired, or motivated others.

6. When you do something wrong, or when something doesn't go as planned, what are the words you often use when talking to yourself?

7. Now that you understand the power of your words, are you ready to choose your words wisely? Create a few empowering words or Word Filters you can choose instead.

    Example:
    1. "I'm a beginner at ____ and that's OK."
    2. "Well, that didn't work out. Let's try_____ instead."
    3. "I know I can do better with practice."
    4. "I'm ready to dedicate time toward achieving my goals."

5. Create three to four Word Filters you can use in the future.

CHAPTER THREE

The Power of Your Body

Your body is one of your most powerful Inner Superpowers. Your body is how you represent yourself (how you "show up" or appear) to the rest of the world.

Your body position, your facial expression, and how you move your body tells others so much about who you are. Even before people have a chance to get to know you, they will have already made a lot of assumptions about you based on your physical appearance and how you carry yourself.

When you understand the Inner Superpower of Your Body, you can show up as a warm and confident person who people are excited to meet and get to know. When I'm talking about the Inner Superpower of Your Body, I'm not talking about how you're dressed or the size of your clothes—although they could support you in feeling good about yourself. Your true power is in how you control your body.

How you move your body has the power to influence your moods dramatically. Therefore, it has a significant impact on your experiences. In the past, it was commonly believed that our minds were fully responsible for controlling our bodies, therefore our actions. In recent years, Embodied Cognition,[1] a newer field of cognitive science (the study of the mind), emerged to show that "the mind is not only connected to the body, but that the body influences the mind." What this means is that our minds influence our bodies, and our bodies influence our minds.

The findings within Embodied Cognition research are so exciting because it helps us to understand the very important roles our bodies play in influencing our moods, actions, and experiences. When you understand how simple these concepts are, you will be able to tap into the Inner Superpower of Your Body to quickly and instantly destroy your fear and self-doubt while boosting your confidence level.

In simple terms, your mind, or the thoughts and feelings you have, influences how your body reacts. Likewise, the actions and positions of your body influence how you feel, which, in turn, affects your thoughts, actions, and experiences.

Why Your Body is a Superpower

To fully understand the power of your body, let's talk about two very key concepts, the Mind's Programs and the Body's Programs.

The Mind's Programs

Have you ever noticed that when you're feeling an intense emotion, such as sadness, everything around you, including

---

[1] McNerney, Samuel. A Brief Guide to Embodied Cognition: Why You Are Not Your Brain "http://blogs.scientificamerican.com/guest-blog/a-brief-guide-to-embodied-cognition-why-you-are-not-your-brain/

the small things that you typically wouldn't even notice, can cause you to feel even worse?

This is because whenever you have a certain emotion, your subconscious mind will automatically run the corresponding "mind's program" for that emotion. A mind's program can be thought of the same way as a computer program, which is a set of procedures or commands for your mind to carry out. The purpose of these emotional mind's programs is to give you—and enhance—the experience you've asked for.

In a previous chapter, you learned that your thoughts and feelings are direct commands to your subconscious mind: "This is the experience I want. Give me this experience." When you are feeling sad, you're giving your subconscious mind the command of, "I want to feel sad. Give me this experience." Your subconscious mind will immediately run your mind's program for sadness.

With the Mind's Program for sadness running, your subconscious mind will look in your movie library and find movies from your past that caused you sadness and start playing those movies in a repetitive loop. This brings those past events back into your awareness, causing you to re-experience the pain from those events again.

You stay stuck in your head, thinking about all these different painful events and your sadness persists. Perhaps you're thinking about a certain mistake you've made repeatedly. Perhaps you're thinking about all the times people have rejected you and caused you pain. Or perhaps you're thinking about all the times you've let yourself or someone else down.

At the same time your old movies are playing in the background, your subconscious mind will scan your environment, looking for evidence for why you should be sad. Anything that has the potential of making you feel sad will be picked up by your subconscious mind and pointed out to you. You become hyperaware of the things that make you sad, while the things that could make you happy get completely ignored.

Each time you play your mind's program for sadness and experience sadness, your beliefs about sadness and who you are in relation to sadness become stronger. You feel trapped within this loop, which could make you feel as though you are powerless against these repetitive thoughts. These negative, reoccurring thoughts can even lead you down a path of greater sadness and create feelings of anxiety, hopelessness, or even depression.

As if that's not bad enough, your subconscious mind will take another step to enhance the experience you've requested. Using the evidence it has picked up on from your past movies, your subconscious mind will create a new movie for you. Only this time, it is set in the future. In this movie, you are still trapped in the repetitive patterns that caused your sadness—you're still letting yourself and others down and people are still rejecting and hurting you. This little gift from your subconscious mind helps to keep you in the experience you had asked for.

This is a very common path for the mind's program for most emotions. When you are in a particular emotional state, your subconscious mind will do everything it can to continue or heighten that feeling for you. It will replay your past movies, look for external evidence, and project similar events into your future. The net result is that you get to continue experiencing more of those same feelings.

Remember, you asked for the experience and your subconscious mind is just doing its job and being a good assistant to you.

The Body's Programs

Your body also has its own programs for your various emotions. To simplify, I will call them the "strong body program" and the "weak body program."

Typically, when you feel anxious, inferior, scared, or another similar negative emotion, your body will run the "weak body program." When the weak body program is running, you and your body tend to close up. Your shoulders might start feeling heavy or tight and your gaze might start going downward. You might start slouching, crossing your arms or legs, or even curling yourself up into the fetal position. When you feel bad about yourself or your situation, your body naturally becomes smaller, as if to hide or protect you from any real or perceived danger.

The opposite is true for when you are feeling self-assured, happy, or powerful and you are running the "strong body program." When you feel good about yourself, your body naturally opens up and your gaze is either focused ahead or upward.

A study[2] comparing blind Olympic athletes (some who were blind at birth) with athletes who can see normally shows how dramatically similar the athletes moved their bodies in response to winning or losing an event. "The winners tilted their heads up, smiled, lifted their arms, clenched their fists

---

[2] Yong, Ed. Blind Olympic athletes show the universal nature of pride and shame. http://phenomena.nationalgeographic.com/2008/08/13/blind-olympic-athletes-show-the-universal-nature-of-pride-and-shame/

and puffed out their chests, while slumped shoulders and narrowed chests were the hallmarks of losers."

Isn't that interesting? Even the athletes who were blind from birth and who have never witnessed another person's body movement would display the same body movements in response to winning or losing. This is because we are born with these automatic body programs for our feelings, and they are almost identical from person to person.

Think of a time when you aced a difficult test, scored the winning point for your team, or were chosen to participate in something you were really excited about. How did you react physically? Perhaps you gave your friends high-fives. Perhaps you jumped up and down or danced. Or perhaps you puffed out your chest and threw your hands up in the victory position. Every one of those actions demonstrates your body's program for positivity and success. When you feel good about yourself, your body naturally opens up and takes up more space as if to say, "Look at me!"

Similarly, think of a time when you did something that you were really embarrassed about or ashamed of. How did your body react? Did you make direct eye contact with those around you? Did you stand there with your hands on your hips and proudly display your embarrassment or shame, or did you slink away hoping to go unnoticed?

The Mind's and The Body's Program at Work

Let's go back to the mind's program for sadness to show how the mind's and body's programs work together. Once you've triggered the mind's program for an emotion, it runs on autopilot. Your body reacts accordingly by triggering the matching body's program.

Let's say you got into a fight with a friend and now, you're feeling sad. Your sad mind's program kicks in. You start to think about all the other times this friend has caused you pain. Your thoughts might shift to other people who have hurt you and other sad events from your past. You might even think about how this friend will hurt you again in the future.

At the same time, your body naturally responds by closing up. Your energy closes in; you cross your arms over your chest, curl yourself up in a little ball, or become listless. You might even feel mentally, emotionally, and physically drained. You don't want to do anything or talk to anyone. You just want to lie there, curled up in your misery.

All of this happens simultaneously because your mind and your body are working together, running their individual programs, to bring you the experience you've asked for, which, in this example, is sadness. Suddenly, you went from feeling a little sad to feeling very sad. If you do nothing about it and allow these programs to run, you will continue to stay sad.

Here's where it gets really exciting! Your mind and your body have to run the same program for you to continue to stay in your current emotional experience. This is really important, so let me say it again.

Your mind and your body have to run the same program for your mind to continue its path and hang onto your current emotional state.

When your mind and your body are not running the same program, your mind gets confused. When your mind gets confused, it stops running the current emotional program and your feelings change. In this way, your body is very powerful in its ability to influence your feelings.

How to Destroy Fear and Self-Doubt Using the Power of Your Body

How can you use this information to boost your confidence and destroy your fear and self-doubt?

Let's say you're feeling anxious and your mind's program for anxiety is running and causing you to think and remember more anxiety-inducing events. Your body reacts accordingly and kicks in the body's program for anxiety. You notice your body starting to close in and that you have crossed your arms. You notice that you're looking down toward the ground and you're shifting uncomfortably where you're standing.

When you notice your body closing up, what if you decided to tap into your Inner Superpower of Your Body and do something different? Instead of allowing your body to close up, what if you decided to open it up? What if you stand tall and strong, throw your arms up, look up at the sky, and smile the biggest, most confident, or even goofy smile you can imagine? How do you think you would feel if you just changed your body like that?

Let's do a quick exercise to show you what this looks like. Start by standing up with your feet hip-width distance apart. Tighten up your leg muscles and feel how strong your legs are. Stand up tall and look straight ahead and smile the biggest smile you can. Also, either place your hands on your hips or throw them up toward the sky.

How do you feel when you hold your body this way? What happens to your self-confidence level?

For the sake of this activity, go ahead and do the opposite. Start slouching your body, allow your shoulders to become heavy, cross your arms, and look down at your feet. As a bonus, bite your lip lightly while shuffling your feet.

How do you feel in this position? What happens to your self-confidence now? Go back and forth between these two poses and pay attention to the words you're using to yourself and how you feel differently as you move from one pose to another.

Now, imagine yourself walking into a social setting and seeing a stranger standing tall, smiling warmly, and making eye contact with you. What kind of assumptions will you make about that person solely based on how they are presenting themselves with their body? Will you see them as confident, friendly, and approachable?

Next, imagine shifting your eyes and seeing someone else sitting by herself on a bench with her head held down and her arms folded firmly across her chest. What assumptions will you make of her? Does she appear confident, friendly, or approachable?

Now, think about the people whom you thought were so lucky because they seemed confident, easygoing, and well-liked. How do they look? How do they hold their body?

To appear more confident and easygoing, all you have to do is use the Inner Superpower of Your Body. Your body affects not only how you feel about yourself but also how others see you and the impression they make of you.

You have the power to take control and run your positive and successful body's program whenever you want to. It's as simple as the exercise you just went through. When you take on a powerful pose when you're anxious, it confuses your mind because this is not your body's program for anxiety.

REMEMBER: When your mind and body are not running the same program, your mind gets confused. When your mind gets confused, it lets go of that current emotion. You are then free to choose a new emotion that better suits your needs at that moment.

The net result is that you get to break the cycle of feeling like a victim to your emotions and instead reclaim your true power at the moment.

The next time you go into a situation that causes you fear or self-doubt, use the Inner Superpower of Your Body. Instead of slouching in your chair, looking down at the table, and wringing your hands as you're sitting in class, anxiously waiting for your turn to give your presentation, sit up straight.

Use the Inner Superpower of Your Body to relax your shoulders and allow them to drop comfortably. Uncross your legs, turn your knees outward, and plant your feet firmly on the ground. Look directly ahead of you or at the line where the wall and ceiling meet.

The simple act of focusing your energy and attention on keeping your body open and strong will break your negative emotional state and help you to look and feel a sense of confidence instantly. You can then choose the Word Filters you want to create the experience you're looking for.

Self-Reflection

Spend a few minutes answering these questions and coming up with examples for the following:

1. When you are nervous, scared, or tense, how does your body naturally react?

2. When you feel good about something you've just done or about yourself, how does your body naturally react?

3. List two specific examples of a time when your body closed up and caused you to feel even worse about your situation.

4. List two specific examples of a time when your body opened up and caused you to feel good about your situation.

5. Think about the people you admire. How do they hold their body in stressful situations? What could you learn from them?

6. Think about the people you admire. How do they look that tells you they are comfortable with themselves? What could you learn from them?

CHAPTER FOUR

The Power of Imagination

For a moment, think about an early childhood memory when you spent numerous hours playing with your imaginary best friend, having fun in your imaginary land, and doing exactly what you wanted to do.

If you didn't have an imaginary friend, think of a time when you were reading a great book and got completely lost in a make-believe land or immersed in the adventures you were reading about. Or maybe think of a time when you were sick in bed and instead of being bored, you used your imagination and turned your bedroom into a jungle gym or a space station ready to blast into outer space!

Stop reading this book for a few minutes; as vividly as you can, bring back one or more memories of a fun childhood experience. Take your time doing this exercise so you can get the full experience of this next Inner Superpower.

Check in with yourself. As you imagine these events from your past, how do you feel? How is your body positioned? If you took the time to vividly recall one of those wonderful memories, chances are you're feeling a little light-hearted, the fun memories are bringing a smile to your face, and your body is naturally open.

You might not have known it when you were younger, but in those moments, you were using your Inner Superpower of Imagination to create your own amusement and entertain yourself. You were also using your Inner Superpower of Imagination to recall those wonderful memories just now.

Why Imagination is a Superpower

Imagination helps you to entertain yourself, but what is imagination exactly, and what else is imagination good for?

Imagination[3] is defined as "the act or power of forming a mental image of something not present to the senses or never before wholly perceived in reality." It is also defined as "the ability to confront and deal with a problem," and "a creation of the mind."

Based on these definitions, you can see why Imagination is an Inner Superpower. With your imagination, you have the ability to create mental images of something that doesn't even exist in reality—something no one may have ever seen or even thought of before!

With your imagination, you can create endless journeys and adventures that entertain you and bring you excitement and happiness. Imagination gives you the ability to look at different angles of problems and come up with alternative solutions that satisfy you.

When you tap into your Inner Superpower of Imagination, you have the ability to fill your life with fun activities that

---

[3] "imagination." Merriam-Webster.com. 2017. https://www.merriam-webster.com (7 November 2017).

bring you joy and creative solutions that fills you with a sense of adventure or accomplishment.

You use your imagination all day, but probably thought little about how incredible your imagination is. You might even downplay the powers of your imagination with, "I don't have a good imagination," or "It's only in my imagination."

If you think you don't have a good imagination, you are giving your subconscious mind the command, "Make sure to look for evidence that I'm not imaginative." Being your loyal assistant, your subconscious mind kicks in to give you the experience you just requested.

You were born with this precious gift and you have a great imagination. If you didn't have a good imagination, you wouldn't be able to recall past events. It's with your imagination that you're able to "see" your friend's face or feel their warm embrace long after you have parted ways. It's your imagination that helps you decide how to solve fun things, such as puzzles or games, to more serious things such as how to patch things up after you've hurt someone.

You have been using your imagination and the power of your mind all along. You just didn't know how powerful your imagination is, nor how to use it consistently to create the results you want. But that's about to change.

How to Destroy Fear and Self-Doubt Using the Power of Your Imagination

Did you know that it is entirely possible to destroy your fear and self-doubt by tapping into the Inner Superpower of

Imagination? From her studies[4], Dr. Stephanie Carlson, a prominent scientist who specializes in researching how our brains work, determined that with repetition, you can become the person you pretend to be.

What this means is that if you want to be confident, you can become confident by pretending to be confident. To pretend, you have to use your Inner Superpower of Imagination.

Remember, one definition of imagination is "forming a mental image of something not present or never before wholly perceived in reality." When you imagine yourself confident, you are just forming a mental image of yourself in a way that you haven't been before (or haven't consistently been before.)

Think of all the amazing things in your life that you enjoy so much, such as your smartphone, a game console, or even your favorite shoes. For those things to come into reality for you to enjoy, someone had to first imagine them. And not only does someone have to imagine them, but they also have to imagine them in a positive way, a way that brings excitement into that project. Without imagination, nothing would ever get created.

It is no different for you. If you want to be a certain way, you can use your imagination to bring that version of yourself to life. You can use the power of your imagination to see yourself as a fully confident version of yourself.

How do you look? What are you saying? Who are you with? What are you doing? You can use your imagination to

---

[4] Carlson, Stephanie M. et al Evidence for a relation between executive function and pretense representation in preschool children. (2014) https://www.ncbi.nlm.nih.gov/pmc/articles/PMC3864685/

vividly see yourself going after what you want with confidence and achieving your goals with ease. Notice how good it feels to just imagine that possibility.

Here's another fun detail about your subconscious mind that helps you bring the things you imagine into real life:

Your subconscious mind doesn't know the difference between real or imagined events. To your subconscious mind, your real or imagined events are just programs. As a program, it's either on or off.

If you're thinking it, feeling it, or doing something, your subconscious mind will view it as a current event that is happening at that moment.

When you vividly imagine yourself tackling a problem with confidence repeatedly, your subconscious mind will believe that you have been successful at tackling that problem with confidence many times. If you have been successful in overcoming a problem ten or twenty times, will you still have the fear or self-doubt the next time you face that problem?

Not likely.

However, if there is still some doubt, you can change that by imagining the successful completion of that task easily and with confidence another twenty—or hundred—times.

Here's another fact about your subconscious mind that is important to create your desired outcome. In an earlier chapter, you learned that your subconscious mind is very literal and will obey your command in the easiest, quickest way possible. When you use the power of your imagination, be sure to use present-tense terms.

This looks like: "I am confident in who I am," instead of "Once I'm confident in who I am, I will..."

When you say and imagine, "I am confident in who I am," you bring your goals of being confident into the present moment. Your subconscious mind will hear and obey the command: "I am confident now. Give me the experience of being confident now."

When you say, "Once I'm confident in who I am, I will..." you're telling your subconscious mind, "Give me the experience of being confident... someday. I want to be confident at some point in the future."

You might say, "I'm OK with being confident someday. It doesn't have to be today." While that's fine to feel that way, imagine what it would be like to take control and change now.

Besides, your subconscious mind will need you to give this command consistently to rewrite your old programming. Now is the perfect time to take those first steps in making your permanent change.

Am I a Fraud?

I'm sure you have heard the expression, "Fake it till you make it." There's a lot of truth to that statement according to Dr. Stephanie Carlson's research[5]. However, for many people, the

---

[5] Carlson, Stephanie M. et al Evidence for a relation between executive function and pretense representation in preschool children. (2014) https://www.ncbi.nlm.nih.gov/pmc/articles/PMC3864685/

idea of faking something or pretending to be someone they're not, feels dishonest and wrong.

Many times, I've heard clients say, "I don't want to lie to myself. That is just not right." or "I feel silly pretending to be someone I'm not." When you fake it till you make it, you can look at it as "pretending, lying, or deceiving," or you can look at it as "practicing."

When you go to the gym and work out with weights, are you tricking your body into developing muscles? Of course, you're not! You are actively participating in activities that result in your muscles being developed. You are, practicing with weights to strengthen and build your physical muscles.

Imagination is a mental muscle. Instead of thinking of it as tricking yourself or lying to yourself, how about changing those Word Filters to "practicing," "strengthening," or "developing" your mental muscles? Doesn't it feel good to actively engage in developing your physical muscles?

You can look at your mental muscles the same way and allow yourself to feel good each time you practice this new skill. With repetition, your beliefs become stronger and more developed, and your brain chemistry changes to match.

Your Personal Creation Studio

Here's a fun way to view your imagination. Think of your imagination as your Personal Creation Studio, or "Studio" for short. Your Studio is your private playground, a place that is safe for you to test out and practice anything you want to develop, whether that's a skill or a thing you want to create.

If you want to develop a certain trait or create a new thing, you can go into your Studio and try out different ways of bringing that goal to life. The cool thing about your Studio is that it's your own private place where you are free to try and try again until you're happy with your result.

In your Studio, there is no pressure; there is no judgment. If you get a result you don't like, you can adjust different aspects of it, or you can scrap it altogether. Your Studio is equipped with a "do-over" button that you can use as many times as you want. You have full control of what happens here!

Let's say you have a fear of talking in front of a group of people and you want to change that. You can start by going to your Studio and practicing visualizing yourself walking up to a group of people, smiling, and saying "hi." Imagine the people you've just approached smiling and saying "hi" back. Do that a few times to feel more comfortable.

Next, imagine yourself standing in a group and being fully present. This means you're not in your head, trying to come up with things to say. Rather, you are there, listening to the conversation and enjoying the moment.

Now, imagine yourself adding to the conversation and imagine the people responding back positively. If you imagine these scenarios repeatedly and you feel good when you imagine them, how do you think you'll be different in a real social setting?

Here's a hint that will help you be successful in social situations. When you are actively listening to a conversation, it is much easier to have something to say because you are hearing what is being said and can respond appropriately.

When you're in your head, thinking about what to say, it feels forced and unnatural. By the time you come up with something to say, the conversation has already moved on and what you came up with may no longer be appropriate, making you look or feel awkward.

REMEMBER: *Your subconscious mind doesn't know the difference between real or imagined events.*

If you're in your head, thinking about being laughed at for saying the wrong thing, your subconscious mind will think you just, in fact, had that experience.

Similarly, if you took the time to imagine yourself at ease and having fun in a social situation twenty times, your subconscious mind would believe that you had fun in a social situation twenty times—twenty actual events where you were at ease and confident while hanging out with others.

When you actually interact with a group the first time in real life, your subconscious mind will think this is the twenty-first time that you've interacted in a group. Since the first twenty times were so wonderful, your subconscious mind has no reason to "protect" you with fear or doubt. Thus, you get to relax and enjoy your time.

With each time you imagine yourself successful, you strengthen your mental muscles and build up the skills necessary for you to be comfortable in a social setting. The best part is you did that all in your Studio, where there are no risks, only opportunities to practice!

The problem is that many people don't understand the enormous power of imagination. Rather than using their Studio to empower themselves, they use it to practice being someone they don't want to be and create scenarios that are damaging to their emotional and physical health.

Before they go into a social situation, they would imagine going to a party where everyone knows each other, and they are the only one who doesn't know anyone. Or they might imagine themselves being the only one who is nervous and awkwardly saying the wrong things and being laughed at or ignored.

This, of course, further increases their fear, anxiety, and self-doubt. By the time they get into that social situation, their anxiety level is so high that they do, in fact, look and act awkward. Their body closes in, they shift uncomfortably, and they can't make eye contact with people.

Similarly, some people spend so much time in their Studio reliving past painful events that it causes them to experience physical symptoms of stress. This interferes with their sleep, their ability to focus, and decreases the overall quality of their lives. They created all of this because they didn't understand the power of their imagination. Anytime you catch yourself creating unwelcomed situations in your Studio, know that you have the power to stop that now.

Remember, your subconscious mind is always paying attention to your commands. When you think or feel a certain way (and you do this using your imagination), your subconscious mind will do all it can to give you the experience you're creating in your Studio.

Your imagination has a very important and vital role in helping you solve problems and be happy. When you actively engage your Inner Superpower of Imagination and use your Studio to practice being the person you want to be, you will change how you feel about yourself and how you feel about your world. You will see problems from different angles and come up with new ways to approach and solve those problems.

Here's a key point to remember:

In every situation, you have to focus your energy and attention on something, whether that's a negative, neutral, or positive aspect of that event. Your mind cannot be completely blank. Why not focus your attention on something that will make life easier and more fun for yourself?

Self-Reflection

Spend a few minutes answering these questions and coming up with examples for the following:

1. Think of the last time you actively engaged the power of your imagination, whether by watching a movie, reading a book, or just creating something great in your mind. How did you feel?

2. Think of a time where you allowed the power of your imagination to get the best of you and become fearful or full of self-doubt. What were you imagining? How did you feel?

3. Go into your studio and come up with two different ways you can think about the situation you just mentioned. Remember to engage your Inner Superpowers of word and your body along with your imagination to create new, powerful scenarios. Have fun in your Studio. Your new scenarios could involve fairies, werewolves, unicorns, and superheroes if you like. Remember, this is your private playground. Have fun and tap into your imagination. How do you feel now, having imagined the situation in a different and positive light?

The Power of Courage

When you think of the word "courage" and someone who is courageous, what comes to mind? Who comes to mind? Do you envision someone jumping out of an airplane into enemy territories in the middle of the night? Do you imagine someone scaling a towering, icy mountain or scuba diving with sharks hundreds of feet below? Do you think of someone standing up against a group of hostile people, pushing back and fighting for social change or human justice?

For many, this is how they view courage. To be courageous, many think they must accomplish a nearly impossible task filled with risks of personal injury or even death. It's these epic events that get celebrated in the media and talked about non-stop around the dinner table or among a group of friends.

When compared to these courageous heroes, many people feel bad about themselves because they have trouble thinking about getting out of bed and facing the day, let alone taking those types of enormous risks. Too many people get trapped in this way of thinking, which causes self-doubt, fear, and negative self-judgment.

Maybe you are caught in this pattern, too, and you don't know how to stop feeling bad about yourself or your situation. Once you understand true courage and how to tap into your Inner Superpower of Courage, how you view yourself and what you are capable of will dramatically change for the better.

Why Courage is a Superpower

Courage[6] is defined as "the ability to do something that frightens one," and "the mental or moral strength to venture, persevere, and withstand danger, fear, or difficulty."

Simply put, courage is the strength and ability to face something that YOU see as frightening, difficult, or dangerous. To be courageous, you do not need to climb Mount Everest, tame wild beasts, or stand up against a firing squad. To be courageous, you only need to stand up and face the things YOU are afraid of and find difficult.

Based on these definitions, you are courageous. You are much more courageous than you've realized and much more courageous than you've given yourself credit for. In the words of Nobel Peace Prize winner Nelson Mandela, "I learned that courage was not the absence of fear, but the triumph over it.[7]"

Think about that statement and then think about the countless times you took a step toward something that completely frightened YOU.

---

[6] "courage." Merriam-Webster.com. 2017. https://www.merriam-webster.com (7 November 2017).

[7] https://www.brainyquote.com/quotes/quotes/n/nelsonmand178789.html

How about that time you could finally strike up a conversation with someone you found intimidating? Maybe your heart pounded rapidly, and you stumbled on your words, but you did it. And even if the results may not have been what you wanted; the fact is that you found the courage to face your fear at that moment.

What about the time you stood your ground and said what you wanted to say? Yes, it was scary, and perhaps you might have even second-guessed yourself for speaking your mind, but the fact is you did. You courageously did it! You looked directly at your fear and went for it! This, in and of itself, is an incredible act of courage that went unnoticed by the world around you— and it probably even went unnoticed by you.

You have been courageous so many times in your life, but you just haven't given yourself the proper credit and acknowledgment. You don't have to let these incredibly courageous moments go unnoticed anymore. You can recognize them, celebrate them, and in doing so, increase your connection to your courage and how often you engage this Inner Superpower throughout your day.

Each tiny, seemingly insignificant act of courage you undertake strengthens your self-belief and stretches the boundaries of who you are a little more. When you start to notice and celebrate these wins, however small they might be, you feel good about yourself.

Remember, your subconscious mind is always paying attention to your thoughts and feelings to know what type of experiences you are looking for. When you celebrate these wins, your mind takes notice. It will look for more evidence to show you just how courageous and capable you really are.

You feel more self-assured. You begin to see yourself differently. You start to think and act differently. You allow yourself to take more chances and do the things you want to do because you trust yourself more.

The courage and confidence that grow out of these seemingly unimportant events begin to take shape. You become more and more comfortable challenging yourself and pushing yourself to achieve even greater goals. The things you once thought were big roadblocks become possible and your goals for even greater success are now within reach.

Courage opens up your world; the possibilities are endless. True courage is acting when you feel fear and it is also listening to and following your heart. Courage is accepting yourself exactly as you are. Courage allows you to push through when life gets tough. Courage allows you to connect to others in a deep and meaningful way.

It takes courage—lots of it—to allow others to see your vulnerabilities, your scars, and your quirks. It takes courage to dream big and pursue that dream until it becomes a reality. It takes courage to move on from situations or people that are toxic and unhealthy for you.

When you tap into your Inner Superpower of Courage and face your fear, you become unstoppable.

How to Destroy Fear and Self-Doubt Using the Power of Courage

Many people have so much fear and self-doubt that they can't relax and be themselves. They work hard to avoid the people and situations they are frightened of. They are always on high alert, watching their environment, looking for danger. They continuously try to be the person they think others want them to be. This constant need to be vigilant about their situation and the self-imposed need to figure out who they need to be in each moment amplifies their fear and self-doubt.

Imagine having to guess what each person expects from you and then trying to act in such a way to meet their expectations with every interaction you have. How exhausting would that be?

With each person you try to impress, you pretend to be the person you think they want you to be, and you lose a little more of yourself. Soon, you lose connection to who you really are and the beauty and uniqueness that is you fade away. This leaves you even more confused about who you are. How can you be confident and courageous when you don't even know who you are and what you stand for?

The same goes for always being on guard for potential situations that could bring you pain or disappointment. Imagine not being able to relax in any situation because you are continually looking for your escape route. Instead of being present and enjoying each moment, you stay trapped inside your head, thinking of all the things that could go wrong so you could "prepare" yourself. The harder you try to control your environment and those around you, the less you feel comfortable in your own skin and the more fear and self-doubt you'll create.

When you practice acts of courage, you can eliminate the need to control your environment and the need to change yourself to please others. Courage will allow you to be yourself and to be genuinely comfortable in your own skin.

Here's a little fact you may not know about that will instantly help you live more courageously:

Fear exists only in your imagination. Fear is created by recalling events from the past or imagining events in the future. Fear does not exist in the present moment.

Therefore, if you turn all of your attention on being in the present moment, you instantly eliminate your fear.

"Wait!" you say. "I'm always afraid. Fear is with me every moment, even in the present moment!"

Let's look at those statements a bit to see if they are really true. First, think of the last time you were fearful. What thoughts were running through your mind? Let's pretend that you had a class presentation, and you were afraid. You probably had some, if not all, of these thoughts:

1. I will be so nervous.
2. I will forget what I need to say.
3. I will make a fool of myself.
4. People will laugh at me.
5. I will get a bad grade.
6. I'm terrible at public speaking.
7. I've made a fool of myself in the past.
8. I'm just too scared.

Let's look at the first five statements. These statements are based in the future. These are things you are afraid of and you're hoping to avoid them in your future.

Statements six and seven are based on your past experiences. You believe you are a terrible public speaker because of how you presented in the past, and you view that event as you making a fool of yourself.

You might say that statement eight is based on the present moment and you are somewhat correct. "I AM" is a present-tense statement; however, when you go deeper and ask, "why are you scared?" the answer will either be based on a future event ("I'm scared because I might fail.") or based on your past experiences ("I'm scared because I've done poorly in the past.").

Instead of letting your past experiences and fear of the future control your reactions, what if you tapped into your Inner Superpower of Courage to stay in the present? It takes courage to let go of old familiar patterns and start down a new, unknown path.

As you're sitting in your chair, waiting for your turn to present, instead of entertaining those old fearful thoughts, what if you just focused on the moment? Maybe your classmate, Amie, is giving her presentation and you focus all of your attention on what she's saying. Maybe Amie is wearing a shirt with a cool pattern and you spend your time mentally tracing the outline of that pattern.

Maybe you can spend your time taking slow, deliberate breaths and focusing on your Inner Superpower of Words to boost yourself up or opening up your body to stay calm and confident. Maybe you use your Inner Superpower of Imagination and mentally practice delivering your presentation with confidence. When you courageously stop the old chatter in your mind and do something positive for yourself, you'll improve your outcome drastically.

Remember, having courage does not mean that you have no fear. Rather, it means looking at your fears and taking actions to overcome them. The best way to strengthen your Inner Superpower of Courage is by doing something courageous.

It might seem very counter-intuitive to say, "I don't have the courage to do the things I want to do, but I'm will do it anyway because I want to be courageous."

You might think, "That's easy for you to say because you don't have my problem. You don't know what it's like to be me and live with my fear. You don't know how much I've already suffered."

While it is completely true that I do not know your unique circumstances, I do know that we all struggle with our own challenges, fear, and self-doubt. I also know that courage is a skill that you can learn to master with patience and practice. I'm not suggesting that you take your biggest fear and tackle it head-on. That method might backfire and reinforce your belief that your fear is justified and impossible to overcome.

Courage is another mental muscle. It gets better with constant use. To exercise your muscles for courage, start small and build your courage muscles up along the way. Find little ways to push yourself or expose yourself to new things every day. It might feel awkward at first to do something outside of your comfort zone. The more you continue to push past your comfort zone, the more your comfort zone will expand.

Let's say that singing is a passion of yours and something that you're really good at. You may want to pursue this as a career, but the idea of performing in front of others terrifies you. What small steps could you take to overcome your fear?

Perhaps the first step is singing a few songs to your family. Perhaps it's singing to a group of your close friends. For some, it's easier to do the thing they are afraid of with people they don't know. If this is you, maybe you can look for opportunities to sing to a small group of strangers? Could you look for opportunities to sing at a daycare or a nursing home? Gradually increase the size of the group and the duration of your performance until you feel at ease performing for an audience.

REMEMBER: You can practice and perfect all of your courageous acts within the safety of your Studio before doing it in real life.

With continued practice, courageous acts will become second nature to you and your confidence will become more and more obvious in the way you live.

Self-Reflection

Spend a few minutes answering these questions and coming up with examples for the following:

1. Think of three different times where you were acting courageous but did not give yourself the proper credit. Write down all the relevant details.
2. As you consider the events you wrote about in question one through the lens of courage, how did it make you feel differently?
3. Think about each event again individually. For each event, is there something you wished you would have done or said differently? Write those things down.
4. Next, pick one of those events to practice with. Imagine going into your Studio and reacting the way you wish you had. Practice this way of being repeatedly until it feels comfortable to you. This exercise will help you to react in this way in your future. Feel free to practice reacting the way you want with the other events, too.

CHAPTER SIX

The Power of Forgiveness

How often do think about the times you were hurt, mistreated, or rejected by others? When you replayed those events in your mind, how did it make you feel? What emotions came up for you?

Chances are when you thought of these events, you felt several strong emotions such as sadness, fear, hurt, disappointment, betrayal, inferiority, anger, powerlessness, loneliness, shame, or other equally negative feelings. Has it ever helped you to feel this way? For most people, the answer is "no."

In fact, you've probably experienced having your entire day ruined, not because of what happened that day, but because you spent so much time and energy feeling sorry for yourself or beating yourself up for what you should have or could have done differently. You wish you could let things go easily like others around you, but you can't seem to stop thinking about what happened and how people have hurt you. How can you forgive and move on when you can't stop reliving the pain in your head?

You are not alone in this pattern. As humans, it's easy for us to focus on and replay negative events. In fact, we are wired that way. Our life experiences have taught us to pay extra attention to negativities and hang on to the pain associated with them.

Ever since you were a little child, you have watched the people around you giving more attention to negative events and giving you the impression that negative events are worth paying special attention to.

Think about it for a moment.

There were countless times where you were happy playing by yourself and no one took notice. But the moment you hurt yourself, hurt someone else, or did something "bad" like throwing a tantrum, everyone around you rushed in to give you extra attention. Yes, some of that attention was negative, but it's still attention all the same.

Further, when something terrible happens, people talk about it more. If it's newsworthy, every channel on TV will broadcast the story repeatedly. You can't seem to get away from the story no matter how many times you've changed the channel.

Whether or not you know it, events like these cause your subconscious mind to develop beliefs such as, "When I get hurt or do something bad, I get extra attention," or "Pain, trauma, and other unfortunate events are important. Pay attention to them." So, when something goes wrong or when someone hurts you, you hang onto those memories and replay them often.

Think of a time when you had a horrible experience at a restaurant. How many people did you share that experience with? What about a time when your restaurant experience was just so-so? How many people did you share that experience with? More likely, you told at least twice as many people about the negative experience as compared to the OK experience.

When you think about those two restaurant examples, how many details can you recall about each incidence? You are likely to recall many details from the terrible experience and not so many things about the so-so experience. This is because your mind is wired to pay attention to and remember negative events.

Remember your friend and assistant, the subconscious mind? It has a vital role in keeping painful memories fresh in your mind. Since its job is to keep you safe from danger (real or imagined), your subconscious mind will not only remember all of your painful experiences, but it will also continuously scan your surroundings for evidence of similar wrong doings to prompt you to avoid certain people and situations.

Sadly, this causes you to be hypersensitive to each instance where you perceive that people might mistreat you, or when you think you are doing something "wrong." This often leads you to misread situations and creates unnecessary pain for you.

Why Forgiveness is a Superpower

Stress is the number one cause of so many health problems, such as high blood pressure, stomach problems, headaches, and depression. When you carry so much fear, doubt, or anger, whether at yourself or others, your stress level increases, and it affects your overall health.

Forgiveness is a key to lowering your stress and improving your quality of life.

Forgiveness liberates you from all that heavy burden (and subsequent stress) while providing you with a clean slate to move forward.

Imagine this scenario for a moment. You just got into a terrible argument with a good friend, and you feel like she was mean and hurtful to you. You tried to explain to her why you're feeling hurt and upset, but she just doesn't seem to get it. You become angrier as you withdraw inside yourself. Your friend is trying to make light of the situation and says, "Stop being so sensitive. Come to my party tonight. We'll have so much fun."

If you're hanging on to the hurt, chances are you would choose to stay home and not attend her party. You might even think, "I'm going to send her a clear message about how angry I am by not showing up to her stupid party."

So, instead of going to the party and having fun like you really wanted to, you stayed home and stewed in your anger and misery. Your friend, on the other hand, proceeded to have a great time at her party. She might think about you briefly and she might even feel sad for a moment that you're not there, but she most likely will be focused on the friends who are there and enjoying her time with them.

You wanted to make her pay, but in the end, who really suffered? You were so wrapped up in your pain and thoughts of making her pay that you couldn't enjoy yourself. You replayed the fight over and over, which caused you to be even more upset with your friend. You might even become so irritable that you yelled at your little brother when he asked you to play with him. You are now the one dishing out the pain and you didn't even realize it. How damaging is that?

Let's imagine that you decided to forgive your friend instead. It might feel a little awkward at first because you're not used to letting things go easily. However, because you have learned how to unleash some of your Inner Superpowers, you went into your Personal Creation Studio and practice these new skills.

For thirty minutes straight, you practiced hanging out with your friend at her party, being fully present, and having fun. You practiced seeing yourself completely at ease, laughing with and connecting deeply with this friend and other friends at her party. As you practiced these new skills in your Studio, you also practiced a new ISP Command: "It's easy for me to forgive."

With these practices, you began to feel better about the situation and decided to attend her party. At the party, you noticed how much easier it was for you to have fun. Your friend was thrilled that you attended the party. She gave you a big hug and thanked you for being there.

You leave the party feeling good about yourself and your friendship, and you bring that wonderful energy home with you. When your little brother asks you to play with him, you do so happily, and you two share a precious bonding moment.

Inspirational author Katherine Ponder[8] said something that I very much agree with, "When you hold resentment toward another, you are bound to that person or condition by an emotional link that is stronger than steel. Forgiveness is the only way to dissolve that link and get free."

When you choose to forgive, you stop wasting your time and energy rehashing the same old story and feeling sorry for yourself. That's the power of forgiveness.

---

[8] http://www.azquotes.com/author/20507-Catherine_Ponder

REMEMBER: *When you forgive, you set yourself free to enjoy the things that matter most to you.*

You might think, "OK, that makes sense, but what if I forgive someone and they don't change because they think I'm OK with what they did? Or worse yet, what if I forgive them and they think I'm weak and they take advantage of me even more? I don't want to be friends with someone like that."

While it's understandable that you might have these concerns, would you agree that these concerns are fear-based? If you want to destroy your fear and self-doubt, you can choose to shift your energy away from the familiar fear-based thoughts and focus on your Inner Superpowers instead.

When you forgive, it doesn't mean that you have agreed with what happened, nor does it mean that you've excused their actions. All it means is that you've accepted that the situation occurred and there's nothing you can do to change the past, so you're choosing to focus on the present moment and the future.

Maybe it's a simple misunderstanding and you can quickly clear things up by having a meaningful conversation that deepens your relationship. Maybe there's a great lesson or two that you can learn from to help you grow as a person. When you forgive, the act of forgiveness is really for you and not so much for the other person.

Yes, it would be nice if they can understand what they did and change their future behavior because of it. However, the decision to change is entirely up to them. You have no control over that, regardless of how much time, energy, and effort you spend trying to make it happen. The more you try to control or manipulate the situation, the longer you stay trapped and bound to this person. It's almost as if you gave them the power to control how you feel.

Instead, you can forgive that person and move forward. In doing so, you reclaim your power. It's like you're declaring, "Enough! You can't control me anymore. I'm in charge of how I feel and how I spend my time."

Forgiveness also doesn't mean that you have to be friends with that person. Just as the other person has the choice whether to change, you have a choice in whether you want to maintain that relationship. Forgiveness just means letting go of the negativity so you can move forward, with or without that person in your life.

So far, we've been talking about forgiving others and how that frees you. Let's talk about another side of forgiveness that is equally important, but often overlooked, and that's self-forgiveness.

For a moment, think of something you did that you still feel regret, guilt, or shame about. Or maybe think of a time when you let yourself or someone else down, or somehow disappointed yourself. How do these events and the feelings attached to them hold you back? Does it feel heavy and burdensome to carry all of those self-judgments around with you? Wouldn't it be nice to start fresh and move forward without that burden?

If you want a fresh start, you can begin by forgiving yourself. Just like forgiving others, forgiving yourself does not mean that you are OK with what you did. Self-forgiveness means you've recognized that what you did was not desirable and you're willing to let it go so you can spend your energy on discovering ways to improve that situation or make up with someone that you may have hurt.

How to Destroy Fear and Self-Doubt Using the Power of Forgiveness

How does forgiveness help you destroy your fear and self-doubt? Holding onto feelings of hurt, anger, or resentment only makes you feel worse about yourself and your situation and ultimately causes you to second-guess and doubt yourself. You might feel like a victim. You might feel all alone in this world. It's no wonder that you would want to protect yourself from future pain.

But what happens when you try to defend yourself? Usually, self-protection means thinking about and remembering the act that caused you pain, hoping to avoid a repeat event. It also means having to close yourself up to some degree.

Maybe you've been rejected or betrayed by a friend, so now, you're afraid to open up and let people get to know the real you. Perhaps you've been teased by others for expressing yourself, so now, you hold back from saying what you want to say. Perhaps you've failed at something important to you and now, you no longer attempt to take on meaningful challenges out of fear of repeating the failure.

Let's say you've been picked on by a classmate and now, you're afraid to be around that person. What thoughts do you have when that person is near you? Do you show up as a happy, confident, and carefree person? Or do you show up as angry, timid, and awkward? Are you showing up in a way that makes it difficult for someone to tease you, or are you showing up as an "easy target?"

I'm not suggesting that it's your fault that they teased you. You are definitely NOT at fault. Bullies will be bullies, and you cannot control that. What you do have control over is how you feel and how you present yourself to others.

Remember, your subconscious mind is always working to give you more of your current experience. When you focus on how this person has teased you and caused you pain, your subconscious mind will look for evidence of the same. This causes you to be on high alert and fearful.

Remember the chapter about the Inner Superpower of Your Body? In that chapter, you learned that when your mind is running a "weak mind program" such as fear, your body will naturally close up, making you look small and not very confident. These factors work together against you, making it easier for bullies to continue to pick on you. The good news is that you can change this pattern.

Imagine you've forgiven the person who picked on you and let go of the negativities. Rather than taking what they said or did personally, you recognize that this person is dealing with their own stuff and was just taking it out on you. That doesn't make the situation right, but it puts the situation in a different perspective for you, doesn't it? How would you show up differently now? What thoughts would you have?

The next time you see that person, rather than feeling fearful, you might feel neutral or better yet, even compassionate toward them. Because you are no longer focusing on fear, your mind and your body will respond appropriately, and you will appear completely different to others.

When you focus your energy on protecting yourself, you limit your positive energy and limit your ability to be in the present moment.

REMEMBER: Fear exists only in your imagination. You create fear by recalling events from your past or imagining events in your future. Fear does not exist in the present moment.

When you get out of your head and focus on what is in front of you, you eliminate your fear and self-doubt. When you don't have to worry so much about how to act, what to say, or how to protect yourself, you will feel better and stronger overall. Your self-esteem and confidence automatically increase. You can relax, be yourself, and enjoy the people around you and the environment that you're in.

In addition, forgiveness can help you develop and strengthen your other Inner Superpowers and restore your peace of mind. How powerful is that?

NOTE: Forgiveness work can be challenging for many. While the following exercises are helpful in releasing unwanted emotions, they do not replace professional help. If your situation is difficult to handle, or you don't know how to proceed on your own, please talk to your parents or a trusted adult and ask for help.

You can also do an internet search for "teen crisis" with your city and state for local resources. For example, "teen crisis Asheville North Carolina."

Self-Reflection

Spend a few minutes answering these questions and coming up with examples for the following:

Forgiving Others

1. Think of a person or situation that you still hold anger or resentment for. Write down key relevant information.
2. How is holding on to the negativity and pain from this event holding you back? What has it prevented you from doing? What might it have caused you to do that you otherwise wouldn't have?
3. Are you afraid that something bad would happen if you were to forgive this person or situation? Go ahead and express any fear you might have.
4. How can forgiving this person or situation improve your life? What are you now free to do, think, or feel without the weight of this issue?
5. Take a moment to notice how liberating it feels to let go of the weight of this problem. With your forgiveness, you have the power to give yourself this magnificent gift of freedom to move forward.

Forgiving Yourself

1. Think of something that you've done that you feel regret, guilt, or shame about. Write down all the relevant details.

2. As you were thinking about and writing down details of that event, how did it make you feel? What thoughts did you have?
3. Why haven't you forgiven yourself?
4. What are you afraid would happen if you forgave yourself?
5. What can you learn from this event?
6. How can you use what you've learned to help yourself be a better person?

Spend a few minutes envisioning this improved version of yourself, having learned a powerful lesson. Give yourself permission to embrace this lesson and move forward now.

CHAPTER SEVEN

The Power of Love

L ove is a primary and essential human need. There are thousands of songs about love. There are thousands of movies about love. Human lives are conceived as a result of love. Love conquers all. Love makes the world go 'round.

There is no shortage of inspiration for words to describe love and the effects of love. Without love and nurturing, we can't thrive. We crave the feeling of being loved and we enjoy showing love to those we care about. Love fills us with a sense of comfort, belonging, and safety. When we have love, life is easier and more meaningful. When we lack love, life seems lonely and cold.

Let's do a quick check-in on the love you have in your life. Stop reading this book and for the next five minutes, grab a piece of paper and make a list of all the people you love. Take the time to create this list before continuing with the rest of this chapter. This is an important step to assessing your Power of Love. Go ahead; grab a piece of paper and a pen or pencil. Set your timer for five minutes and go! Just create your list freely and write down whoever comes to mind.

Take a look at your list. At what point did you mention yourself? Are you toward the top of your list, somewhere in the middle, or at the very bottom? Did you even make it on your own list?

It is common for people to forget to include themselves on their "People I love" list because they focus their love outwardly. When they think of giving and receiving love, they think it's an act coming from themselves to someone else or from someone else to them.

Others feel uncomfortable with the idea of self-love, fearing they might appear arrogant or self-centered. Still, others feel unlovable or see themselves as being undeserving of self-love.

Where are you on this spectrum? Do you show yourself the same level of kindness, love, and respect that you show others, or do you treat yourself poorly in these areas? Do you make time for yourself as you do for others?

While it's a wonderful trait to love others and to treat others with love, it is equally, if not more important to love yourself.

To fully experience the Power of Love, you need to start from within and develop a strong feeling of love for yourself. In this chapter, when we talk about love, we're talking about self-love. When you love yourself deeply, giving love to and receiving love from others will be a breeze.

Why Love is a Superpower

When you think of self-love, what is the first thing that comes to mind? Do you get excited at the thought of being able to show yourself how important and deserving you are? Or does the idea of taking the time to care for yourself and your needs feel foreign and uncomfortable for you?

If it puts a smile on your face when you think about showing yourself love, then you're ahead of the curve. Go ahead and continue to show yourself just how magnificent you are!

If it makes you uncomfortable to think of self-love, let's work together to change that. You deserve to love yourself and treat yourself with respect, kindness, and compassion.

Why would something as simple and beneficial as practicing self-love be so uncommon and difficult for many? Part of that answer may lie within our culture's definition of self-love[9]: "1. Conceit 2. Regard for one's own happiness or advantage."

Given that part of the definition of self-love is "conceit" and "regard for one's own advantage," it's no wonder so many people are uncomfortable with the concept of loving themselves. After all, who wants to be seen as a conceited person or one who only regards things for their advantage? Consequently, instead of showing ourselves love and creating our own happiness, we give love to others and we depend on others to give us love and to make us happy.

What if, instead of focusing on those aspects of the definition of self-love, we accepted that self-love is "regard for one's own happiness?"

For the next few minutes, imagine that you have the total freedom to focus on creating your personal happiness. To be clear, when I say, "freedom to focus on creating your personal happiness," I mean freedom to do what you want for yourself, as

---

[9] "self-love." Merriam-Webster.com. 2017. https://www.merriam-webster.com (7 November 2017).

long as you're not purposefully breaking the law or hurting someone else.

What would that look like for you? How would you think, act, or feel differently when your decisions are based solely on your happiness and not pleasing someone else—nor being concerned about what others may think of how you spend your time? How liberating does it feel to leave behind the fear, self-doubt, negative judgment, regret, shame, and guilt?

That's exactly what self-love can do for you. It can fill you with wonderful feelings that motivate you to live your life to the fullest. At a deep level, we all want to feel loved and to know that we are deserving of love. We all want to be able to show ourselves love; so why is it hard for most people to show self-love?

The following three misguided beliefs are often cited as the reasons why many people are uncomfortable making self-love a priority.

Misguided Beliefs

It's Selfish to Focus on Your Needs

Chances are, early in your life, the act of self-love and doing what makes you happy was very natural to you. Imagine these scenarios.

You were blissfully minding your own business and doing what feels good to you, instead of allowing your sibling to pressure you to do what you don't want to do. Your sibling got mad at you and angrily accused you of being thoughtless, inconsiderate, or selfish.

Maybe another time you were scolded because you told your parents you wanted to go to your friend's house as planned, instead of staying home to babysit your siblings. Perhaps your parents yelled at you and told you how disappointed they were with you. They said that a good person would think about others' feelings and would sacrifice their needs to make them happy.

Maybe you were told that you should be ashamed of always wanting things your way. Guilt, shame, and a load of other heavy burdens were placed upon you and you learned just how much that hurts.

Your subconscious mind was paying close attention, as it always does. It recorded this whole painful exchange, and it will use it to help protect you from similar painful experiences in the future. The next time you think about doing what makes you happy, your subconscious mind kicks in to protect you and replays this and other similar movies.

You'll start feeling uneasy as you second-guess yourself with questions such as, "Is what I want really all that important? Am I being thoughtless, inconsiderate, or selfish?"

And as you think about those thoughts and feel the anxiety around them, you decide to do what the other person wanted. And for that, you get rewarded. Your parents told you how proud they are that you're thinking about other people's feelings. They tell you that you're such a good person and rewarded you with extra attention, love, or other tokens of appreciation.

After a few of these incidences, you grew up believing:

- Doing what I want is thoughtless, inconsiderate, and selfish.
- It's more important to make other people happy than to make myself happy.

- When I sacrifice my needs, I am appreciated by others.

You're Not Worthy of Good Things in Life

These beliefs were intensified by other experiences in your life that caused you to feel as though you weren't deserving of good things. Perhaps in the heat of anger, your parents yelled at you to stop wasting time on "useless" things (things that you loved doing) because you should focus on bringing your grades up and helping with chores around the house.

Or maybe you've heard your parents talk about all the sacrifices they have made to provide for you and your siblings, and that made you feel guilty. Maybe a friend or two ended their friendships with you because you didn't do what they wanted to do.

Then there were all the times you beat yourself up for messing up or letting yourself or others down. Experiences like these reinforced your belief that your desires and needs are not that important and that you are not worthy of them. To conform to what others expect of you and earn the title of being "worthy," you focus your attention on meeting others' needs while neglecting your own.

When you continue to ignore your own needs, you lose connection to who you are and to what makes you feel good. This causes your self-esteem to plummet and your dissatisfaction with yourself (and your life) to worsen.

You Are Unlovable Because You Are Flawed

Even when you have the time to focus on your needs, you may have a hard time showing yourself love because you can't stop focusing on your perceived flaws. This causes you to feel unworthy and undeserving of love and happiness.

Here's a common scenario among teens. See if you can relate to this or a similar situation. There is a special occasion coming up; maybe a school dance or a friend's party, and you're so excited to attend. You found the perfect outfit and your hair looks great. But this morning you woke up with a large pimple on your face.

Instead of admiring yourself for how great you look and focusing on the fun event, you focus all of your attention on the pimple. Instead of being present and enjoying yourself, you're stuck in your head, thinking about your pimple, which causes you to feel insecure about how you look. At the gathering, you find it hard to enjoy yourself because you're certain that everyone is staring at your pimple and judging you.

If you often feel this way, I have some news for you. You're a human being. As long as you're a human being, you'll have perceived flaws. There's just no way around it. If you wait until you think you are perfect before loving yourself, you'll lose out on an incredible opportunity for happiness and fulfillment right now.

Loving yourself does not mean that you believe you are perfect or that you always do things perfectly. Loving yourself means that you choose to accept yourself exactly as you are, flaws, and all.

REMEMBER: *Showing yourself love and being kind to yourself are two of the best things you can do to build your self-confidence and self-esteem and change your life for the better.*

When you love yourself, you release the constant pressure of having to make others happy and the heavy burden of living with endless self-doubt and self-judgments.

Without the pressure, doubts, and judgment, you'll have the freedom and peace of mind to explore things you enjoy, which helps you to grow as a person. When you know who you are and you feel good about yourself, it is much easier to make positive decisions for yourself.

Self-love acts as a natural anti-depressant and a natural anti-anxiety. The more you love yourself and treat yourself with kindness, the easier it will be to tap into your strength and stay calm and clear-minded during difficult situations.

Self-love also makes bouncing back from these types of events easier. When you practice self-love consistently, you'll become a happier, healthier person with a strong sense of self-worth. Your ability to give and receive love deepens because you now see yourself as a good person who is deserving of love.

How to Destroy Fear and Self-Doubt Using the Power of Love

For a moment, think about how you've been treating yourself when your fear and self-doubt are high. Have you been showing yourself love, or have you been showing disrespect or disregard for yourself? In those moments, are the words you're using to yourself supportive and kind, or do you make the situation worse by calling yourself names and berating yourself for your perceived flaws?

Think about the words you say to yourself in these situations. Would you ever say these same words to a friend, a family member, or even a stranger when they are already down on themselves? Would it be OK to talk to others this way?

Chances are, if you're honest with yourself, the answer is an easy NO! It is not OK to speak to others the way you speak to yourself when you're upset. If you talk to others the way you talk to yourself, you wouldn't have too many friends. People would think you're mean, abusive, or a bully.

And yet, somehow, you feel it's okay to talk to yourself in this manner. These kinds of self-talk show a big disregard for yourself and reinforce your belief that you are unworthy or undeserving of love. This is not exactly a great foundation for showing yourself love.

Instead of beating yourself up the next time you feel fear or self-doubt, what if you tapped into your Inner Superpower of Words to give yourself love and support? One way you can show yourself love is to challenge yourself to treat yourself with the same level of thoughtfulness, kindness, and respect that you show the person you love most.

If you can't imagine saying any words to this person, avoid saying them to yourself. If it makes you feel good to use these words with that person, start using those words to yourself. You can choose positive Word Filters such as:

- "Slow down. Breathe. You've got it."
- "I believe in you."
- "Everything will be OK."
- "Let's figure out how to solve this problem."
- "You can do it!"

You can also go into your Personal Creation Studio and practice solving whatever problem you're facing with courage, confidence, and self-belief. Use your imagination to vividly see yourself conquering your problems in several creative ways.

When you practice trusting yourself and your abilities, your confidence skyrockets. You'll find it easier to face your problems and follow your dreams with courage. How you feel about yourself and the words you use when you talk to yourself become highly positive.

With practice, you'll find it easier to prioritize yourself and your needs. Your subconscious mind will help you achieve your dreams by helping you to focus on the important aspects of yourself. You can practice self-love by forgiving yourself and accepting your shortcomings while giving yourself permission to see the best in yourself.

When you show yourself that kind of love, support, and encouragement, how does it feel? What would you be able to do differently?

Besides showing yourself love in moments of fear and self-doubt, what if you showed yourself love daily by choosing activities that relax you, inspire you, and recharge you? When you make the conscious decision to nurture your body, heart, and spirit, you leave very little room left for fear and self-doubt. If you feel good about yourself and you see your flaws or failures as opportunities for growth, what is there to be afraid of?

REMEMBER: *When you treat yourself as a person who deserves love, kindness, and respect, you are showing others how to treat you.*

Engaging in self-care activities daily help you to release your stress, gives you more energy, and helps you to look and feel your best so you can be happy with yourself and your life.

Remember to include some self-love activities that might not feel very fun, but that you know are important for your overall health and happiness, such as eating healthy.

Self-Reflection

Spend a few minutes answering these questions and coming up with examples for the following:

1. In the beginning of the chapter, you created a list of people you love. Did you make it onto your own list? How did you feel when you discovered that showing yourself love is just as important as showing love for anyone else?

2. Think of a time when you felt upset or disappointed with yourself and you used harsh, damaging words as you talked to yourself. What words did you use? What names did you call yourself?

3. How did those words and names make you feel?

4. What was the outcome of that situation? Was it resolved, or does it still linger for you?

5. Now, think about that same situation again; this time, with love and kindness for yourself. Imagine your thoughts and self-talk through loving Word Filters. What words did you choose to speak to yourself this time?

6. How do these words make you feel differently?

7. How do you think the outcome would have been improved if you had spoken to yourself with these words when you first encountered this issue?

8. List two to three things you currently do consistently to show yourself love. They don't need to be grand gestures or even highly time consuming. Using positive and caring self-talk and allowing yourself to learn when you make mistakes are great examples.

9. Create a list of ten things you could do to show yourself love in the future. Remember, even little things you do that are good for you or allow you the space to feel special are great. Anything counts here, no matter how small or how large, as long as you are showing yourself love in the process.

   Example: eat an apple instead of a bag of chips, take a twenty-minute walk after dinner, listen to music, play with your dog, buy yourself something nice, practice ISP Commands, meditate, etc.

CHAPTER EIGHT

The Power of Perseverance

We all have plans that don't turn out as we intend, dreams that fall apart, and changes that are beyond our control. Setbacks, changes, and obstacles are all a part of life—a part that no one can completely avoid.

How do some people face these tough and ever-changing situations and still come out ahead, while others crumble at the slightest thought of such challenges? What is their secret? How do they keep moving forward when others just want to quit when the pressure becomes higher?

The secret ingredient for the people who keep pushing on when things get tough is perseverance. Some people were born with the ability to persevere, and they can power through even the most challenging situations with seeming ease.

Perseverance is defined as "a steady persistence in a course of action, a purpose, a state, etc., especially in spite of difficulties, obstacles, or discouragement.[10]" How we deal with the constant

---

[10] "perseverance." Merriam-Webster.com. 2017. https://www.merriam-webster.com (7 November 2017).

unpredictable events in our lives depends largely on our attitude, our belief systems, and our commitment to ourselves.

Maybe perseverance is not something that comes naturally to you, and the idea of pushing through difficulty sounds downright scary or even impossible to you right now. Luckily for you, perseverance, like all other ISPs, can be learned and strengthened with practice.

Having perseverance can mean the difference between turning your problems into opportunities or allowing your fear and judgments to cause you anxiety and keep you stuck. Given that the average person has challenges and unexpected curveballs thrown at them every day, knowing how to deal with these situations positively will help you move forward rather than becoming held back.

How you view these events will have a significant impact on your quality of life. Instead of seeing your challenges as disasters and wallowing in fear or self-pity, what if you recognized them as opportunities for growth? How would your life be different if you use these challenges as stepping-stones to an even greater success and happiness for yourself?

Why Perseverance Is a Superpower

Did you know that you have persevered through many challenging situations throughout your life? Did you also know that perseverance is actually a very natural part of who you are?

You don't believe me? Let me explain.

When you were an infant, you did not understand how to feed yourself. The first few times you tried to feed yourself solid food, you made a complete mess. Chances are you fed your cheeks, chin, nose, and floor more often than you fed your mouth. But you didn't stop, did you? You continued to push forward and look at you! You feed yourself effortlessly, and mostly, you actually put food into your mouth and not on the floor like you once did.

Then, there are those times you tried to learn how to walk. How many times did you work so hard to stand up, only to fall right back down before even taking that first step? You didn't give up then either, did you? You persevered.

There could be several chapters written—or even a whole new book or two—about all the other things that you have pushed through, which allowed you to become a stronger and better person. You do this daily without giving yourself credit or even noticing most of the time.

How would your life look right now if you had decided at eleven months old that walking was too difficult and that you were too scared of falling and getting hurt again? Chances are the freedom of movement that you now enjoy and take for granted as a natural part of your being wouldn't be available to you.

I know this example might seem ridiculous at first, but this situation is not very different from the challenges you may face right now. Think about it. At eleven months old, walking was a very difficult and overwhelming task. Your muscles were not fully developed, nor were they strong enough to support your weight effortlessly. You were just learning how to control your motor skills.

The task of controlling your body that is now so automatic to you required much concentration and effort on your part at eleven months old. It required a tremendous amount of effort to just push yourself up from the floor. In the beginning, each time you got up, you fell right back down.

But you persisted.

And don't forget the countless obstacles—the chairs, the coffee table, the slippery floor—all of which made walking ever so challenging. But each time you fell, you brushed yourself off and tried again. You were determined to figure it out and eventually, you did!

At first, you could only take a wobbly step or two before falling again. But you stayed the course. Soon, your steps became solid, and they rapidly evolved into walking longer distances. Ultimately, you even learned how to run.

You might laugh at this example, but that's the power of your perseverance at work. If you had given up on yourself at eleven months old, your life would have been dramatically different— and in this extreme example, be filled with significant challenges.

Not only does perseverance help you achieve your goals and build your confidence and self-worth, but when you persevere, you become healthier mentally.

Spend a moment thinking about how you were affected by a change, challenge, or setback that you worked hard to avoid. What was that experience like? Did you think about it so much you frequently felt worried, tense, or irritable? When you focused so much of your attention on the thing you wanted to avoid, did you have the mental ability to relax and enjoy yourself? Did you feel so anxious that it was hard for you to focus or to sleep well? How about your relationships? How were they affected when you were filled with stress? How satisfied were you with your life at that moment?

Focusing so much on the problem or what's wrong in your life wreaks havoc on your mental health. When you focus on the present moment and on your strengths, you lessen your stress, and your mental health improves.

I'm not saying that once you've decided to persevere, everything will magically fall into place and become easy. You will still have to put in the work to create the changes you desire and some of the work could be boring or difficult for you.

However, when you face your fear and work toward overcoming your problem, your attitude about it changes. Remember, your subconscious mind is always looking for the next command from you and it will do all it can to give you the experience you ask for.

When you think of a situation as overwhelming or as something scary to run away from, your subconscious mind will scan your environment and focus on all the details that could reinforce your feelings of overwhelm and fear. This will make your situation appear even more intimidating.

What experiences would your subconscious mind help you focus on when you think of the same situation with an attitude of, "I have no idea how to solve this, but I am determined to figure it out!"? In this instance, your subconscious mind would focus your attention on ways to solve your problem. Instead of bringing only challenges or obstacles to your awareness, your subconscious mind starts showing you available options. As you begin to see solutions and possibilities, your stress level drops, and your confidence rises.

Perseverance helps you to focus on the big picture while staying in the present moment. Remember, fear is based on your thoughts of the past or future. Being present helps you to release your fear and self-doubt. You can then relax and focus on your strengths, come up with creative solutions, and be open to and accepting of new opportunities.

Things that used to stress you out and cause problems for you in the past don't have to be problems anymore. They can be a great opportunity for growth if you let them.

REMEMBER: Life will continue to throw you curveballs. How you respond to them will determine your outcome and your satisfaction with life.

How to Destroy Fear and Self-Doubt Using the Power of Perseverance

The good news is that tapping into your Inner Superpower of Perseverance is easier than you think. In fact, if you've read the chapters in this book in order, you already know everything you need to know to persevere.

You can cultivate a strong sense of perseverance just by using the power of words alone. However, when you incorporate all the Inner Superpowers you've learned, this task becomes much easier. All you have to do is practice what you've learned so far and you will succeed.

For the next few minutes, think of an obstacle you're facing that seems difficult to overcome. Pay attention to the thoughts you're having and how they make you feel. Think of all the reasons you've been telling yourself why this obstacle is so difficult to resolve.

Maybe you've attempted to solve it a few times but haven't succeeded. Or perhaps you haven't tried to address this problem yet because your fear and self-doubt are too high. Whatever the reason might be, can you see that maybe your inability to solve this issue stems from a lack of self-confidence that prevented you from taking the next step of action and pushing through?

Unleashing your Inner Superpower of Perseverance starts with a powerful mindset of "I believe in myself. I know I can handle anything that comes my way."

But what if you don't believe in yourself and you doubt your ability to handle tough situations? That's OK. Even if you don't fully believe in yourself just yet, know that if you decided to tap into your Inner Superpowers, you could build your self-confidence and self-trust.

Since a powerful mindset is the foundation for perseverance and for achieving any goal, you can start out by tapping into your Inner Super-Power of Words and choose Word Filters that build yourself up. How you think, feel, and act are direct results of the Word Filters that you choose.

Take a step back and look at the whole picture. Examine the Word Filters you have been using when you think about the situation. How can you change those words to neutralize them and make them non-threatening to you?

Pay attention to how you've been judging yourself and the people involved. Doesn't it feel heavy and burdensome to carry those feelings with you? You can release that unnecessary weight and give yourself a fresh start by tapping into your Inner Superpower of Forgiveness.

Forgive yourself for the things you may have done (and the things you could have done but didn't do) that you feel contributed to this situation. Those things are in the past and you can choose a different path moving forward. You can also choose to forgive others and free yourself from that old bond to them that held you back.

Examine the Word Filters you have been using when you think about yourself and your abilities. If you have been using Word Filters that tear you down, you can stop doing that now. Instead, start focusing on your strengths and the things you're good at, even if these things are not related to this particular challenge.

Be kind to yourself by using Word Filters that build up your self-trust, self-confidence, and self-esteem. Tap into your Inner Superpower of Love and do things that relax you, energize you, or motivate you to be your best. Remember to incorporate the Inner Superpower of your Body into your daily life. How you present yourself will strongly influence how you feel about yourself and the situation. Practice holding your body in strong and open positions to increase your confidence.

To persevere, you also need to know your goal. Maybe you don't have the exact outcome in mind and that is fine. You can still take the next step if you know the direction you want to head and have a milestone or two in mind.

Look at the obstacle again. What results do you want to create? Do these results match your values or what's important to you? Do you feel good when you think about achieving these results? Create a plan for overcoming your roadblocks and transforming them into opportunities for growth. Tap into your Inner Superpowers of Courage and Imagination and practice achieving your goal with ease.

Remember, you can practice any of these steps in the safety of your Personal Creation Studio until you feel good about them.

REMEMBER: *When you focus on your strengths and take small, consistent steps toward your goals, you'll build up your confidence and your ability to persevere will become stronger every day.*

You already know how to persevere. You've been doing this ever since you were an infant. All you have to do is put one foot in front of the other, one baby step at a time, and you will stretch and grow in ways you couldn't have predicted or imagined.

Self-Reflection

Spend a few minutes answering these questions and coming up with examples for the following:

1. Before reading this chapter, did you know that perseverance is a very natural part of who you are and that you have persevered through many challenging situations? How does knowing that make you feel differently about yourself?

2. Think of a time when you faced a challenging or difficult situation, and you gave up. What Word Filters did you use? How did they hold you back?

3. Look at the Word Filters you wrote for question two. How can you change those words to neutralize them and make them non-threatening for you?

4. Think about three instances where you persevered despite challenges. Write the relevant details down.

5. Examine the three scenarios you wrote down. What qualities or strength did you embrace that allowed you to keep going? What Word Filters did you use? Write these down. These qualities and strengths will help you persevere in future situations.

Congratulations on completing the action steps to Unleash Your Inner Superpowers to achieve your goal.

You are the key to your success! Whenever you need a bit of inspiration, motivation, or courage to proceed ahead, go back and review the Self-Reflection activities of each Inner Super Powers. Take special care to revisit your Studio to invigorate yourself and recharge your battery with these fantastic feelings.

You now have everything you need to Unleash Your Inner Superpowers to destroy your fear and self-doubt, conquer your goals, and create that epic life you've been dreaming about.

BONUS

Five Simple Steps to
Release Your Unwanted Emotions

Step One: Identify Your Feeling

To take control of your feelings, you must first be able to identify it. Are you feeling sad, disappointed, irritated, or angry? Maybe you're feeling insecure, worried, or anxious? Be as specific as you can with your unique feeling and avoid generalizing everything as "mad," "sad," or "bad." Instead of saying "mad," get specific. Are you angry, hurt, disappointed, or irritated? For this example, let's say you're feeling scared.

Step Two: Rate Your Feeling

Once you've identified your feeling, rate it on a scale of 0 to 10, with 10 being the strongest it could be. For example: "I feel scared, and it's rated 8 out of 10 (which shows you are feeling moderately to severely scared)."

Step Three: Locate Your Feeling

Next, identify where in your body you physically feel this feeling. For example, "I feel scared, and I notice that feeling in my stomach."

Step Four: Identify Your Physical Sensation

Pay attention to how your body responds and describe the sensation you notice. Maybe you feel some tightness, heaviness, or pain. Perhaps it's a dull ache or a burning sensation. Maybe it feels difficult to breathe, or you feel choked up. For example, "I feel scared. It's rated 8/10, and it feels like a sharp pain in my stomach."

Step Five: Releasing Your Negative Feeling

Your breath is powerful and can help you let go of your negative emotions quickly. Let's use the example of *"I feel scared. It's rated 8/10, and it feels like a sharp pain in my stomach,"* to demonstrate how to release your emotion with your breath.

Start by closing your eyes and for a moment, allow yourself to feel the sharp pain in your stomach. Notice how uncomfortable that sharp pain is. Notice how the sharp pain is holding you back from having a good day.

Then, take a very slow and deliberate deep breath in as you count from one to four. As you're counting slowly, imagine that you are collecting the sharp pain with your breath. Next, hold your breath for a count of four to contain your emotion. Finally, on purpose, choose to release the pain with your exhale. Breathe out fully and loudly, letting that pain go as the air leaves your body.

Take in another slow deep breath in and imagine yourself collecting even more pain. Hold your breath once more for a count of four and again, release the pain by breathing out even more deeply and loudly than before.

After two deep and deliberate breaths, allow your breathing to become easy and natural. With every easy breath you take in, imagine yourself picking up more pain. With every easy breath out, you're choosing to release the pain.

As you continue to breathe easily, collecting and releasing your negative emotion, give yourself these ISP Commands: "I choose to let this pain (insert your negative feeling here) go. It feels good to let this pain (your negative feeling) go. I deserve to let this pain (your negative feeling) go. I deserve to be free (or a different positive emotion of your choice)."

After a minute or so, reevaluate your feelings. How do you feel now? Is that old feeling still there, has it changed into a different feeling, or is it still the same feeling, but much less in intensity? Perhaps it is now a two instead of an eight. You might even find yourself pleasantly surprised to find that old feeling had simply vanished.

If you still have any negative sensations, note its location and rate it again. Then, take another two to three deep breaths just as before, collecting and releasing the negative emotions as you do. Continue this exercise until you no longer feel your negative feeling. Your goal is to be free of the negative feeling and take control of your emotions. In the beginning, it might take you several minutes. However, the more you practice, the faster and easier it will be!

You can use this exercise to release any unwanted emotions, regardless of where they came from, not just when you are practicing your ISP Commands.

About the Author

Dear Reader,

If you are a teenager struggling with high stress, anxiety, self-doubt, low-confidence or depressive symptoms, I want you to know that you are not alone. I know because I have been there myself. My name is Jacqui Letran, and I have over eighteen years of experience helping thousands of teens, and I know I can help you!

I know you're frustrated, scared, and lonely. I was too. I also know confidence, success, and happiness are achievable because I have successfully freed myself from those old emotions and embraced my life with excitement, confidence, and joy. My goal is to help you understand the power of your mind and show you how you can master it to overcome your struggles and step into the magnificence of your own being, just like I did—and just like thousands of others have done using these same techniques.

Who am I and why do I care?
My life was rather easy and carefree until I hit my teenage years. Overnight, it seemed that all my friends transformed

from girls into women! They began to wear makeup and dressed in expensive and sexy clothes. They flirted with boys. Some even flaunted the older boys they were dating in front me. I, on the other hand, remained trapped in my boyish body. And, within the rules of my super-strict mother, wearing makeup, sexy clothes, or going on dates were not options for me.

I felt different and isolated—and I quickly lost all my friends. I didn't know what to say or how to act around others. I felt awkward and left behind. I just didn't fit in anymore. I became more and more withdrawn as I wondered what was wrong with me. Why didn't I blossom into a woman like all my friends? Why was life so difficult and so unfair?

- **I blamed my mother for my problems.** "If she weren't so strict, I would be allowed to date and have nice, sexy clothes," I thought. At least then I would fit in, and everything would be perfect!

- **I also felt very angry.** My life had taken a turn for the worst—but no one seemed to care or even notice. I started skipping school, began smoking, and getting into fights. I walked around with a chip on my shoulder and an "I don't care" attitude.

- **I felt invisible, unimportant, and unworthy.** Deep down, I only wanted to be accepted as I was. I wanted to belong. I wanted to be loved.

I thought my wishes were answered when I was sixteen. I meet a man five years older than me. He showered his love and affection on me and made me feel as if I was the most important person on earth. Six months later, I was a high school dropout, pregnant teen living on public assistance. I felt more alienated than ever before. Everywhere I went, I felt judged and looked down upon. I felt despair and was certain my life was over. I had no future. I knew I was destined to live a miserable life.

I felt truly alone in the world.

Except I wasn't alone; I had a baby growing inside me. The day I gave birth to my son and saw his angelic face, I knew that it was up to me to break this cycle of self-destructive thoughts and actions.

That's when everything changed!

I began to read every self-help book I could get my hands on. I was on a mission of self-discovery and self-love. I began to let go of the old beliefs that prevented me from seeing myself as capable, intelligent, and beautiful.

The more I let go of those old beliefs, the more confident I became, the more I accomplished. It was a powerful lesson in how changing my thoughts resulted in changing my life.

Six years later, at twenty-three, I earned my master's degree in nursing and became a Nurse Practitioner. Since then, I have dedicated over eighteen years of my life working in adolescent health. I love using my gift and passion to empower teens to create a bright future for themselves.

As I reflect on my painful teen years, I realize how I played a major role in determining my life experiences. My low confidence had paralyzed me from taking action, thus reinforcing my misguided belief that I was different or inferior.

I knew I had to share this knowledge to help teens avoid some of the pain I had experienced.

In my twenty-plus year career specializing in Adolescent Health, I have:

- Established, owned and operated Teen Confidence Academy, specializing in helping teens overcome stress, anxiety, and depressive symptoms without medication or long-term traditional therapy,
- Established, owned and operated multiple "Teen Choice Medical Center" locations,
- Become a Speaker, Podcaster and Author,
- Educated and supported thousands of teens and adults to overcome stress, anxiety and depressive symptoms,
- Raised a loving, intelligent, and confident man (he is my pride and joy), and
- Completed post-graduate training in holistic and alternative health and healing methods.

I am deeply passionate about helping teens let go of their barriers to see the beauty and greatness within themselves. I believe each of us deserves a life full of health, love, and happiness. I also believe that every person has within them all the resources needed to achieve a beautiful and fulfilling life.

When I was going through my troubled teen years, I needed a place where I could be mentored, where I could learn, reflect, and grow; a place where I could heal and get a proper, healthy perspective of myself and the world around me. I didn't have that option then, or at least I didn't know where to find it.

That is why I became a Mindset Mentor specializing in teen confidence, and that's why I am writing this book for you now.

Thousands of teens are living in quiet desperation right now because no one has shown them the key to their success. My goal in writing this book is to teach you about your mind so you can control your thoughts, feelings, and actions. You can take charge of creating the life that you want and deserve. You deserve to be successful and happy in life. Let's make it happen!

Jacqui Letran

Connect with Me

I love hearing from my readers.
Please feel free to connect with me at:

Amazon.com/Author/JacquiLetran

www.JacquiLetran.com

Facebook.com/JacquiLetran

Linkedin.com/in/JacquiLetran

Instagram.com/JacquiLetran

You can also contact me at:

Author@JacquiLetran.com

Free Book Club Visits

If your book club reads any of the three books from the *Words of Wisdom for Teens Series*, I would love to attend your club's meeting virtually to answer questions you or your members might have.

You can book your free 30-minute spot by emailing me at Author@JacquiLetran.com. Please put "Free Book Club Visit" in the subject line.

Words of Wisdom for Teens Series
Award-Winning Guides for Teen Girls

5 Simple Steps to Manage your Mood
A Guide for Teen Girls: How to Let Go of Negative Feelings and Create a Happy Relationship with Yourself and Others

5 Simple Steps to Manage your Mood Journal
A Companion Journal to Help You Track, Understand and Take Charge of Your Mood

I Would, but MY DAMN MIND Won't Let Me
A Guide for Teen Girls: How to Understand and Control Your Thoughts and Feelings

Jump-Start Your Confidence and Boost Your Self-Esteem
A Guide for Teen Girls: Unleash Your Inner Superpowers to Destroy Fear and Self-Doubt, and Build Unshakable Confidence

Stop the Bully Within Podcast

After seeing thousands of clients, I noticed a common theme among most of those I help—they are their own biggest bully.

Just pause for a moment and think of the words you say to yourself when you did something wrong or failed at something. Are those loving and supportive words? Would you say those same words to someone you love?

For many people, when they think of a bully, they think of someone outside of them—someone who says and does mean things to cause others pain. Not too many people think about the bully they have within themselves.

I'm on a mission to bring awareness to how damaging this "bully within" can be, and to help people learn how to transform that inner critic into their best friend, cheerleader, and personal champion for success.

Listen to the Podcast at
https://www.JacquiLetran.com/Podcast

CPSIA information can be obtained
at www.ICGtesting.com
Printed in the USA
BVHW042249181021
619223BV00005B/13

9 781952 719103